THE BRITISH EXPEDITION

TO

ABYSSINIA

THE BRITISH EXPEDITION

TO

ABYSSINIA

COMPILED FROM AUTHENTIC DOCUMENTS

BY

CAPTAIN HENRY M. HOZIER

3RD DRAGOON GUARDS

LATE ASSISTANT MILITARY SECRETARY TO LORD NAPIER OF MAGDÂLA

The Naval & Military Press Ltd

Published by

The Naval & Military Press Ltd
Unit 5 Riverside, Brambleside
Bellbrook Industrial Estate
Uckfield, East Sussex
TN22 1QQ England

Tel: +44 (0)1825 749494

www.naval-military-press.com
www.nmarchive.com

Cover illustration:
A column of British and Indian troops, including an Elephant Battery,
make their way down the steep road in the Chetta Ravine.

*In reprinting in facsimile from the original, any imperfections are inevitably reproduced
and the quality may fall short of modern type and cartographic standards.*

PREFACE.

SEVERAL accounts of the British Expedition have been published, which have displayed a far higher literary ability than the following pages can venture to lay claim to. They have, however, been written by those who have not had access to those authentic documents which cannot be collected directly after the termination of a campaign.

The endeavour of the author of this sketch has been to present to readers a succinct and impartial account of an enterprise which has rarely been equalled in the annals of war. In the Abyssinian campaign the enemies to be feared more than the open foe were natural obstacles and starvation. These were successfully encountered and subdued. The difficulties would have been more apparent, had their reduction been less skilful. The danger and possibility of disaster would have been more manifest had they been less carefully guarded against.

The aim of the author has everywhere been impartiality; his object truth.

CONTENTS.

INTRODUCTION.

GENERAL TOPOGRAPHY OF ABYSSINIA . . . PAGE ix

CHAPTER I.
BRITISH EXPEDITION TO ABYSSINIA . . . 1

CHAPTER II.
PREPARATION OF EXPEDITION 46

CHAPTER III.
RECONNAISSANCE OF THE COUNTRY 70

CHAPTER IV.
SIR R. NAPIER AT ZULLA 80

CHAPTER V.
ADVANCE TO ADIGERAT 101

CHAPTER VI.
ADVANCE TO ANTALO 116

CHAPTER VII.
ADVANCE TO ASHANGI 150

CHAPTER VIII.

ADVANCE TO LAT 157

CHAPTER IX.

ADVANCE TO THE TAKKAZIE 164

CHAPTER X.

ADVANCE TO THE BASHILO 170

CHAPTER XI.

ACTION OF AROGI 186

CHAPTER XII.

SURRENDER OF THE CAPTIVES 201

CHAPTER XIII.

CAPTURE OF MAGDĀLA 221

CHAPTER XIV.

DESTRUCTION OF THE FORTRESS 244

CHAPTER XV.

THE RETURN MARCH 254

INTRODUCTION.

GENERAL TOPOGRAPHY OF ABYSSINIA.

AT the time when a British Expedition into Abyssinia was determined upon little was known of the topography of Abyssinia. This little could only be gathered by compilations from the works of a few travellers who had penetrated into the country. Such visitors naturally pay little regard to military necessities. Careful of the safety and welfare only of a small cavalcade or a diminutive following, what would be nothing wherewith to feed a large host appears to them plenty of both food and water. On the other hand, obstacles which seem to their individual powers stupendous fade away before the disciplined labour of an army. Hence, as authorities for military preparation, the accounts of ordinary travellers are of no great worth. Still they have an advantage.

From the published works of those who had journeyed in Abyssinia it was known that that country is a highland plateau elevated on lofty hills above the basin of the Indian Ocean on the east and the Upper Nile on the west. This plateau runs almost due north and south. At its northern end it impinges nearly upon the shore of the Red Sea, and protrudes its lowest spurs in the neighbourhood of Massowah, close down upon the coral-bound coast. The Red Sea trends towards the east, so that although in the direction of Massowah the mountains of Abyssinia approach the water, there is a belt of lowland of about two hundred miles between the southern portion of the plateau and the ocean.

The plateau was known to be broken by deep valleys and precipitous gorges, through which the rain which fell upon its highest peaks drained off towards the Nile. On it were several political divisions, of which the best known were Bogos, Barea, Hamasyen, Tigre in the north; Semien, Bellesa, Begemeder, Woggera, Dembea, and Tschelga in the centre, separated by the river Takkazie from the northern provinces and from Waag Lasta and Amhara on the east. Shoa lay in the extreme south, and Kuara and Damot on the western slope. In an elbow of the river, which rises in lake Tsana and falls into the Nile at Khartoum, are situated the districts of Metcha and Godjam. From three ports in the eastern coast of Africa can an entry be made into Abyssinia. From Massowah on the north routes lead through mountain passes to Adowa, the capital of Tigre, or round the base of those mountains to Kassala and Matamna, whence Gondar, the principal city of Dembea, can be reached. From Amphila Bay a road runs across the low unhealthy desert to the base of the mountains, and striking through some waterless passes arrives at Adowa. Between Tajurrah, the most southern port, and the mountains, the distance is greater than that from Amphila Bay. From Tajurrah the most direct road lies to Ankober, the capital of the kingdom of Shoa. The lowland along the sea-coast was well known to be an arid and sandy desert: the plateau was known to be rugged and mountainous, but while the climate of the lowlands was known to be extremely prejudicial to European constitutions, that of the hill country was believed to be cool and healthy.

THE BRITISH EXPEDITION

IN

ABYSSINIA.

CHAPTER I.

BRITISH EXPEDITION TO ABYSSINIA.

THE British Expedition to Abyssinia was prompted by no thirst for glory, by no lust of conquest. Unwillingly entered upon for the sake of humanity by the Government of England, it was vigorously carried through in the same cause by the officer to whom its conduct was entrusted. Its success was great. England acquired from it no territorial aggrandisement. Yet it did not pass unrewarded, for its result was greatly to raise the British Army in European estimation.

The troops of Sir Robert Napier were not only liberators of their countrymen, but were explorers and pioneers in an almost unknown land. A vague charm was presented to the men who comprised the Expeditionary Force. The theatre of their operations was little better understood than when it was supposed to be the seat of empire of the mythical Prester John, or was charmed into an unreal existence by the magic pen of the author of Rasselas. The cloud of mystery which enveloped the African Switzerland, the certainty of adventure, and the confidence felt by all ranks of the army in the chosen commander, lured many volunteers to seek for service in the enterprise. Apart from the army there was no desire for the expedition. Many were the forebodings of disaster, and of death to the prisoners in case of an armed intervention in the affairs of an uncivilised potentate. These forebodings were not without cause, but fortuitously so, for they were due less to thought than to awe, to calculation than to ignorance.

The country of Abyssinia, or Habesh,* is inhabited by a mixed race. Of this the majority, although settled on the confines of the Negro world, came from the Shemite race, and speaks a language closely allied to Arabic and Hebrew. Thousands of years ago successive migrations of this people must have emerged from Asia, and settled in Alpine Africa, where, though all historical record is lost, a monument of their migration is preserved in the name Geez or 'wanderers.' The ancient Abyssinian tongue was the Ethiopic: while this was preserved there was comparative civilisation in the highlands, which are drained by many fountains of the father of waters. An extensive ecclesiastical literature existed in the country. The modern lan-

---

* *Habesh* signifies 'mixture of peoples' in Arabic.

guage of several dialects is descended from the Geez or Ethiopic, but is contaminated by the proximity of Arabic-speaking tribes.

Of the earliest history of Abyssinia little is known. Still less can be credited. Legendary chronicles tell, that from this district the Queen of Sheba travelled to visit the capital of the Jewish Solomon, returning thence to the seat of her power at Axum, in Tigre, with the ark of the covenant and a Hebrew colony, and there raised a temple to the true God. The mythical traditions still preserved in Abyssinia say, that the royal house of the country has directly descended from the Queen of the South, and the Negoos, or ruler of modern Ethiopia, claims descent from Menilek, an asserted child of Solomon by the Queen of Axum. The invasion of Abyssinia by the Greek Ptolemies, and the penetration of the arts and language of Greece into Tigre, the country of the Axumitæ, are proved by the inscriptions recorded and found at Adulis and Axum. These were executed before the introduction of Christianity. They own the worship of Mars, and also show that Adulis, the modern Zulla, was the door by which the Greeks and Egyptians obtained access to the highlands of Tigre. Christianity was introduced at the beginning of the fourth century by Frumentius, who was consecrated by Saint Athanasius of Alexandria, the first Primate of Abyssinia. He received the name of Abuna Salama, or Father of Peace, from the

Early history.

people to whom he was sent. Since the days of Frumentius every orthodox Primate of Abyssinia has been consecrated by the Coptic Patriarch of the church of Alexandria, and has borne the title of Abuna.

Jews had been numerous in Arabia since the days when the market of Jerusalem was first supplied from Ophir, and the land of spice on the Red Sea. After the destruction of the home of the chosen people, many exiles of Jewish race found an asylum in the peninsula which forms the eastern shore of the Red Sea. Educated to war in Palestine, and smarting under defeat, they were formidable, both as warriors and bigots. Some of them, in the year 522, made a proselyte of Dunaan, who slew and possessed himself of the crown of the Arian king of the Homerites in Yemen. He persecuted those who refused to renounce Christianity, and at Najiran committed some of the recusants to the martyrdom of fire. The oppressed Churches appealed for aid to the Emperor Justinian. At his request their nearest co-religionist, the Negoos * of Abyssinia, took up arms. Caleb or Eleesbam, who then occupied the throne of Axum, passed his army in vessels from Adulis across the Red Sea, slew Dunaan, and took possession of his kingdom. In the time of Caleb the kingdom of the Axumitæ attained to its highest degree of prosperity, and was

Conquest of Yemen.

* *Negoos* signifies 'supreme prince, or leader:' it is the same word as is applied to David in the Old Testament.

most intimately connected with European civilisation. Its vessels from Adulis traded to Egypt and Ceylon. Its ruler's alliance was sought by the sovereign of the Roman Empire. An Ethiopian colony was established in Yemen, over which Abrahah, the slave of a Roman merchant of Adulis, obtained government. But the army of Abrahah was destroyed before Mecca, and the Abyssinian invaders expelled from Arabia. The conquest of Egypt by the Arabs in the middle of the seventh century, crippled the prosperity of Abyssinia. The rising wave of Islamism severed the arteries of communication which connected Axum with the centres of civilisation and of Christianity. Abyssinia sank into torpid oblivion for almost a thousand years.[*]

During this time the religion of the country became degraded and perverted. The Abuna was uniformly sent into Abyssinia by the Patriarch of Alexandria. But the occasional advent of a high priest was insufficient to maintain the national creed, even on so elevated a basis as that of the Coptic Church. Errors rapidly crept in, and Abyssinian Christianity became tainted with superstition and Judaism. The mission of Frumentius appears to have been only partially successful; and probably the Jewish adventurers in Arabia crossed over in considerable numbers to the African continent after the conversion of Arabia

---

[*] The early accounts of Abyssinia are most conflicting, as presented by Bruce, Gibbon, and several other authorities.

to Islamism. The Jews gained strength, and the legends say that, about A.D. 960, Judith, the Queen of the Abyssinian Jews, overthrew the established dynasty. The heir of the Queen of Sheba was carried to the province of Shoa, where the rightful line continued to reign. The relatives of Judith ruled the remaining provinces of the empire under the designation of the House of Zagué. On the death of the foundress of the line, her successor adopted the Christian faith. About A.D. 1268, by the mediation of the Abuna Tecla Haimanout, a treaty was concluded between Icon Amlac, the descendant of the legitimate line, and the representative of the line of Zagué. By virtue of this agreement, the lands of Lasta were given up to Naaculto Laab, of the lineage of Judith, who resigned to Icon Amlac the kingdom of Abyssinia.* About the middle of the fifteenth century, Abyssinia came in contact with Western Europe. An Abyssinian convent was endowed at Rome, and legates were sent from the Abyssinian convent at Jerusalem to the council of Florence. These adhered to the Greek schism. But from that time the Church of Rome made an impress upon Ethiopia.

<small>Communication with Portugal.</small> Prince Henry of Portugal, youngest son of John the Avenger, and Grand Master of the Order of Christ, next opened up communication with Europe.

---

* This account of the internal history of Abyssinia is extracted from Bruce's translation of the native annals.

He hoped to open up a route from the west to the east coast of Africa, by which the East Indies might be reached without touching Mahometan territory. During his efforts to discover such a passage to India, and to destroy the revenues derived by the Moors from the spice trade, he sent an ambassador named Covillan to the Court of Shoa. Covillan was not suffered to return by Alexander, the then Negoos. He married nobly, and acquired rich possessions in the country. He kept up correspondence with Portugal, and urged Prince Henry to diligently continue his efforts to discover the southern passage to the East.

In 1498 the Portuguese effected the circuit of Africa. The Turks shortly afterwards extended their conquests towards India, where they were baulked by the Portuguese, but they established a post and a toll at Zeyla, on the African coast. From here they hampered and threatened to destroy the trade of Abyssinia. Under the advice of Covillan, Helena, Empress of Ethiopia, sent an embassy to seek assistance of the Portuguese against the Turks, and aid in the extirpation of the Moslem on both shores of the Red Sea. Matthew, an Armenian, who was selected for this service, was detained for three years by the Portuguese authorities in India before he was sent to Lisbon by a homeward-bound fleet laden with spice. During the absence of Matthew, the Turks of Zeyla, allied with the Mahometan tribes of the coast, invaded Abyssinia. They were defeated by the Negoos David, and at the same time the Turkish town of Zeyla was stormed and burned by a Portuguese fleet. The Mahometans, not discouraged, silently prepared for further operations, equipped themselves with fire-arms, and trained themselves in the service of artillery. In 1520, a Portuguese fleet arrived at Massowah. Matthew was on board one of the vessels. An embassy from the fleet visited the court of the Negoos, where nearly six years were wasted in puerile efforts at diplomacy and childish wrangling, without benefit to either side. In 1526 the Portuguese mission was dismissed, and sailed to India, taking with it an Abyssinian ambassador. This envoy, Zaga Zaab, after touching on the Coromandel coast, arrived safely at Lisbon, but, pleased with the amenities of European life, did not hurry forward the affairs of his master. The King of Portugal was not now pressingly desirous of the Abyssinian alliance. The power of Portugal in India was consolidated. A free communication existed between Europe and India round the Cape of Good Hope. The successes of the Turks on the shores of the Red Sea little affected the Portuguese. But the intercourse of the Portuguese fleets with Abyssinia alarmed the Turks on the coast, who had strengthened themselves by constant communication with Arabia, had garrisoned Zeyla, and armed that place with a train of artillery.

<small>Portuguese Mission.</small>

A Mahometan army, under the command of Mahomet Gragné, governor of Zeyla, invaded the highlands, burnt Axum, occupied Amhara, and reduced the Negoos David to the most dire necessity. When pressed hard, David persuaded the Abuna to consecrate as his successor, Bermudez, a Portuguese, who had been detained in Abyssinia on the departure of the mission. Bermudez started immediately to obtain the consecration of the Pope, which he received at Bologna, and then proceeded to Portugal to urge for assistance against the Turks. The viceroy of the Portuguese possessions in India was ordered to send a detachment of 400 musqueteers to aid the Christians of Abyssinia. A Portuguese fleet under the command of Stephen da Gama came to the port of Massowah, where they seized by stratagem the town of Arkeeko on the mainland. Stephen da Gama then began to enrol the men who were to form the auxiliary force. It was found, however, that the whole of the Portuguese wished to volunteer for the service. A considerably larger number than the allotted 400 musqueteers were consequently allowed to take part with their servants and followers in the expedition, which was placed under the command of Christopher da Gama, the younger brother of the Admiral.

The Portuguese force marched from Arkeeko towards Dobarwa, the easiest known entrance to the highlands. It had no provision to make for either its commissariat or transport, as cattle for both food and carriage were supplied by the Bahar Nagash or Abyssinian governor of the sea coast. At Dobarwa, Don Christopher met the queen, and then, with his Portuguese and 12,000 Abyssinian warriors, marched forward to effect his junction with the army of the king. Mohammed Gragné, desirous of preventing this manœuvre, marched into the province of Tigre. An action ensued on March 25, 1542, in which the Portuguese repelled the attack of the Moors, but, from the want of cavalry, were unable to follow up their success. The Portuguese then went into cantonments, to avoid the rains. In August they again entertained the idea of effecting a junction with the Negoos in Dembea. Mohammed Gragné threw his army in their way. Da Gama, without awaiting the arrival of the army of the Negoos, accepted battle. His army was overthrown, he himself taken prisoner, and put to death.

The queen, with Bermudez the Patriarch, sought and obtained refuge among the Jews who occupied Mount Semien. Arius Diaz was elected leader of the surviving Portuguese. On February 10, 1543, the Negoos Claudius and Arius Diaz defeated the troops of Mohammed Gragné, who was himself shot in the action by a Portuguese marksman. Quarrels then sprang up between the Court and the Catholic Primate. Bermudez wished the Negoos Claudius to profess himself publicly as a convert to Rome. The latter refused, not so much from want of conviction as from personal dislike of Bermudez; the quarrel progressed until finally the Negoos, availing himself of force, banished Bermudez to the country of the coast, whence he returned to India.

It was at this time, in the middle of the sixteenth century, that the Galla tribes first attracted attention. A migration of Gallas came from the south, and swept up to and over the confines of Abyssinia. Men of lighter complexion and fairer skin than most Africans, they were Pagan in religion and savages in customs. Notwithstanding frequent efforts to dislodge them, they have firmly established themselves. A large colony has planted itself on the banks of the Upper Takkazie, the Jidda and the Bashilo. Since their establishment here they have for the most part embraced the creed of Mahomet. The province of Shoa is but an outlier of Christian Abyssinia, separated completely from co-religionist districts by these Galla bands. About the same time the Turks took a firm hold of Massowah and of the lowland by the coast, which had hitherto been ruled by the Abyssinian Bahar Nagash. Islamism and heathenism surrounded Abyssinia, where the lamp of Christianity faintly glimmered amidst dark superstition in the deep recesses of rugged valleys.

Galla Incursion.

In the year 1556, St. Ignatius, the general of the Society of Jesus, died at Rome. He had founded a religious Order, of which the influence had been felt in

Jesuit Mission.

the furthest corners of the world; and did not neglect to send aid to the fainting worshippers of Christ in Abyssinia Two years after the death of their great master, a Jesuit mission arrived at Massowah five days before the occupation of that place by the Turks. This mission was under the guidance of Andrew Aviedo, who was appointed Patriarch by the Holy See. The Jesuit missionaries in Ethiopia fixed their head-quarters at Fremona, about twelve miles from Adowa. The Jesuits propagated not only religion, but a knowledge of the rudiments of the arts and sciences, amongst their African flocks. For nearly a century Fremona existed, and its superiors were the trusted advisers of the Ethiopian throne. One of the last, Peter Paez, appears to have been the instrument of the foundation of Gondar in the province of Dembea. This city afterwards became the capital of the Negoos. But the same fate which fell upon the company of Jesus in more civilised lands, pursued it in the wilds of Africa. The Jesuit missionaries were universally popular with the Negoos, but the prejudice of the people refused to recognise the benefits which flowed from Fremona. The Catholic priests were, not unnaturally, regarded as enemies and opponents by the national clergy. The Portuguese advisers of the Negoos were looked upon as stranger favourites by the native aristocracy. Religious and social antagonisms sprang up. Persecution, the desire of their first master, fell upon the Jesuits. The ignorant superstitions of the native priesthood were more potent to the popular mind than the adoption of mechanical appliances, or the application of liberal science. On the death of Socinios, his son ordered the patriarch and missionaries from the different provinces to proceed immediately to Fremona. The Jesuits sought the protection of a rebel chieftain, who refused, from a curious scruple against breaking his promise of protection, to deliver them up to Negoos Facilidas, but agreed, nevertheless, to sell them to the Turks. The majority were accordingly sold to the Governor of Massowah. These were ultimately allowed to return to Portugal; two of those who remained in Abyssinia, in desire and expectation of death, had their wishes completely gratified, and received the martyr's crown at the hands of the Negoos.

Facilidas, weary of missionaries and of foreign interference, sent for a Coptic Abuna from Alexandria, and concluded a treaty with the Turkish governors of Massowah and Souakin to prevent the passage of Europeans into his dominions. Some Capuchin preachers, who attempted to evade this treaty and enter Abyssinia, met with cruel deaths. Facilidas thus completed the work of the Turks and the Gallas, and shut Abyssinia out from European influence and civilisation. The religion and morals of his people became rapidly corrupted. The former is now no

Alliance with Coptic Church.

safeguard of morality, and in the hands of Theodore became only an excuse for cruelties and barbarity.

The sacraments of baptism and the Eucharist are celebrated in the manner of the Greek Church, but children are circumcised, and the Mosaic precepts are generally observed as far as religious and not moral rites are concerned. Images are not adored, but as in the Greek Church pictures are enshrined in the religious edifices. Legends of saints appear to form the bulk of Abyssinian literature. After the expulsion of the Jesuits, Abyssinia was torn by internal feuds and constantly harassed by the encroachments of and wars with the Gallas. Anarchy and confusion ruled supreme. Towns and villages were burnt down, and the inhabitants sold into slavery.

Mission of M. Poncet.

Towards the end of the seventeenth century, efforts were made, both by the Franciscans and Jesuits, to institute an Ethiopic mission. At the same time the Negoos Yasous, who, as well as his son, was afflicted with a scorbutic disease, sent a messenger to Cairo to seek a physician. The French Consul despatched M. Poncet, a French surgeon resident in Cairo, who was entrusted also with diplomatic duties, accompanied by a Jesuit, Brevedent. These approached Abyssinia by the valley of the Nile. Brevedent died of dysentery, but Poncet penetrated to Gondar, where he remained for nearly a year. He succeeded in curing the Negoos, but in his political task failed signally. The Abyssinians refused to send a mission to France, and in 1700, Poncet set out from Gondar on his return journey. At the time of Poncet's visit the Negoos was the virtual as well as the theoretical ruler of the whole of the country. Poncet describes Yasous as devoted to war, but averse to bloodshed. This Negoos received the epithet Tallac, or Great, in the Abyssinian annals. A French embassy, under M. du Roule, which was despatched from Cairo in 1704, did not get farther than Sennaar, where the ambassador was murdered.

Yasous was succeeded by his son, Tecla Haimanout, who was assassinated. The brother of Yasous, Theophilus, ascended the throne. He was the first who allowed the dignity of the Negoos to decline. Theophilus raised Ristas, a maternal grandson of Yasous the Great, to the position of Ras, or prime minister, and entrusted him with the government of the two provinces of Semien and Tigre. On the death of Theophilus, Ristas made himself king, but the legitimate line was restored on his decease. Towards the middle of the eighteenth century the Gallas appear to have increased considerably in power. In the intestine quarrels of Abyssinia their alliance was courted by each side, and in their country political refugees obtained a secure asylum. In order to obtain the permanent assistance of these powerful tribes, Yasous II., or Adam Segned, as he is indifferently called, took

Decline of power of Negoos.

a Galla woman to wife. She embraced Abyssinian Christianity, and religious scruples, perhaps, would not have led to any bad effects from the Pagan alliance of Yasous. On his death, in 1753, he was succeeded by his son Joas, a minor, who was completely in the hands of his mother. The absorption of all temporal benefits by the Galla relations of the queen-mother quickly roused the indignation of the Abyssinian nobility. The whole country rallied round Ras Michael, governor of Tigre, who assumed the actual direction of affairs, while the Negoos was maintained as the theoretical ruler of the country, but was in truth a mere *roi fainéant* in the hands of the Ras. In this condition, Bruce found the Negoos Tecla Haimanout II., when he visited Gondar in 1770. After the deaths of Ras Michael and his son, great disorder ensued. The real power of the Negoos and post of Ras fell into the hands of the chiefs of the Yedjow Gallas, who, notwithstanding interruptions, managed to maintain that position for three generations. The Negoos, who lived at Gondar, with a small suite, received little consideration and no respect from the governors of the different provinces. The two districts most remote from the seat of government, Tigre and Shoa, became independent.

Communication with England.

The campaigns in Egypt attracted English attention to the Red Sea. In 1804 Lord Valentia, the Viceroy of India, sent his secretary, Mr. Salt, into

Abyssinia.* Mr. Salt found Ras Walda Selasyé governor of Tigre, who had secured that province on the death of the sons of Ras Michael. Mr. Salt entered into friendly relations with Ras Walda, but was unable to penetrate beyond Tigre, on account of the constant hostilities between the governor of that province and the Ras Guksa, chief of the Yedjow Gallas, who ruled in Amhara. An Englishman of the name of Pearce remained in Tigre, when Mr. Salt returned to England, and took up his residence at Chelicut, a beautiful village near Antalo. In 1810 Mr. Salt was again sent with a mission to Abyssinia, and was the bearer of presents from George III. to the ruler of Abyssinia. The quarrels between Walda Selasyé and Ras Guksa still continued. The English envoy failed to reach Amhara. He gave the presents to Ras Walda Selasyé, and left the country, where Mr. Pearce and Mr. Coffin, who had accompanied the mission, still remained.

On the death of Ras Walda Selasyé in 1816, intestine disturbance occurred in Tigre. After some conflicts Sabagadis, who had been a frequent rebel against Ras Walda, obtained the supreme power. In 1818 Mr. Pearce left Abyssinia, and shortly afterwards died at Alexandria. Mr. Coffin became a trusted adviser and friend of Sabagadis, by whom he was sent in 1828 to Bombay and England to obtain fire-arms. During

Rise of Sabagadis.

* *Travels of Lord Valentia* and Salt's *Abyssinia* are the authorities which have been consulted; as also Dr. Beke's *British Captives in Abyssinia*.

Coffin's absence a league was formed against Sabagadis by the Galla Ras Marye, the son and successor of Ras Guksa of Amhara, and Dedjatch Oobye, the ruler of the province of Semien. In a battle, fought 1830, Sabagadis was taken prisoner and put to death, leaving several sons.* The Gallas occupied Adowa, but on the death of their chief † retired into Amhara, where a boy, Ras Ali, nephew of Ras Marye, was entrusted with the government, his mother being regent.

Dedjatch Oobye, on the withdrawal of the Gallas, assumed the government over Tigre; which was hotly contested by the sons and adherents of Sabagadis. During these quarrels Coffin returned, in 1832, from England with muskets, some of which he gave to the sons of Sabagadis, who, notwithstanding, were forced before long to yield to the superior power of Oobye. Oobye ruled in Tigre until 1855. Constant wars occurred between the different provinces, most of which were now thoroughly independent of Ras Ali, who ruled the central provinces alone. Goshu was chief of Godjam, and Sahela Selasyé independent King of Shoa. During the time of the government of Oobye, several Protestant Missionaries visited Tigre, but were expelled in 1838, when they directed their attention to the kingdom of Shoa. In 1841, a Catholic mission was established in Tigre, under Padre Jacobis, an Italian

---

* See Chapter V.
† Ras Dori, brother and heir of Ras Marye.

gentleman of noble family, who fixed his head-quarters not far from Adigerat. An English embassy was sent in 1841 to the Court of Shoa, of which Sir William Harris was the leader. It had apparently, however, but little result.

The different Abyssinian chieftains appear about this time to have desired to enter into relations with England, possibly with the idea of obtaining aid against each other, or of seeking for Christian assistance against their Mahometan neighbours. In the same year as Harris visited Shoa, Dedjatch Oobye, of Tigre, sent Mr. Coffin on a mission with presents to the Queen. In October 1846, Ras Ali also sent a mission with presents to the Queen by Mr. Plowden, who with Mr. Bell had arrived in Abyssinia in 1843, and had since lived there.* At this time Mr. Plowden reported that the rightful Emperor still resided, a shadow of royalty, at Gondar. Ras Ali represented the race of powerful chiefs, Galla by origin, but now Christian, who had retained the government for about sixty years.

In January 1848, Mr. Plowden was appointed consular agent for the protection of British trade with Abyssinia, and was sent out with a letter and presents to Ras Ali. He was also the bearer of the draught of a treaty of commerce to be concluded between Ras Ali and England. In the beginning of 1849, Plowden

Consul Plowden.

---

* Correspondence respecting Abyssinia presented to Parliament.

reached Adowa and then proceeded to Debra Tabor, the residence of Ras Ali, whence he returned the treaty of commerce signed by the Ras. On his arrival at Debra Tabor, Plowden found his former companion Bell an officer of high position in the service of the Ras. Her Majesty's ratification of the treaty of commerce was delivered to Ras Ali in 1852. At the end of the same year the attention of the government of Debra Tabor was drawn towards the man who rose on its ruins to be the ruler of Abyssinia.

<small>Rise of Theodore.</small> Lij Kassa, afterwards so well known as the Emperor Theodore, was born in Kouara, the western province of Abyssinia, about the year 1818. His father was of noble family, and his uncle Dedjatch* Comfu was the governor of the provinces of Dembea, Kouara, and Tschelga. On the death of his father his mother is said to have been so hard stricken by poverty as to have been obliged to vend the drug kosso for her livelihood. Young Kassa was nevertheless educated to be a scribe or daftera in a convent near lake Tsana, whence he moved to his native district of Kouara, on the convent being stormed and plundered by a rebel chief. On the death of his uncle Kassa was made governor of Kouara by Waizero Menen, the mother of Ras Ali. Finding no sufficient scope for his ambition in Kouara, he occupied Dembea and raised the standard of rebellion. Several generals were sent against him, but Kassa had

* *Dejatch*, 'chief,' or 'duke.'

introduced a kind of discipline among his followers, and had taken the precaution, unusual in Abyssinia, of having his camp watched by sentries and patrols at night. The chiefs sent against him were successively defeated. Waizero Menen herself shared no better fate. On the assurance that he would receive no harm, Kassa visited the capital of Ras Ali, where, in order to insure the attachment of the rising chieftain, the Ras gave his daughter Tavavitch to him in marr'age. During the life of this lady Theodore is said to have been abstemious, humane, sober, and continent. It was after her death that he commenced the course of atrocities and cruelties which caused his name to be execrated in Abyssinia, and his country to be invaded by the foreigner.

After his marriage Kassa returned to his province of Kouara. His religious education had inspired him with a belief that he was destined to be the restorer of the Christian empire of Ethiopia and the exterminator of the Turks and Pagans, who had encroached upon its frontiers. With this view he engaged in frequent crusades against the Arabs and Shangallas in the direction of Sennaar, but was defeated at the head of 16,000 men by a mere handful of Turkish soldiery at Kedaref. This disaster taught him how difficult it is for wild warriors to engage with success even the smallest band of disciplined troops in the open field. Had he enticed the Turks into an invasion of his own province, acted against their communications, and cut off supplies, he might have reduced an army three times as numerous as his own.

In the action of Kedaref Kassa was wounded, and had to halt, on his retreat, in Dembea. The mother of Ras Ali insulted him in his fallen state. On the instigation of his wife, Kassa resolved to avenge this insult. As soon as he recovered from his hurt he proclaimed his independence in Kouara. Several commanders were despatched to subdue him. He defeated them, and their soldiers usually joined the retinue of the rebel. In 1852 he signally overthrew and killed Dedjatch Goshu, one of Ras Ali's best generals. The Ras now took strenuous measures to oppose Kassa's rise: and called upon Oobye of Tigre to aid him. Kassa marched into Godjam, and defeated the allied troops of Ras Ali and Oobye. The former fled for refuge into the Galla country, soon afterwards gave up the contest, and lived in an asylum by Kassa's permission. By this victory, the whole of the possessions of Ras Ali fell into Kassa's hands. He patched up a peace with Oobye, by the conditions of which he obtained tribute and the person of the Abuna. This peace was preserved until Birro Gosho, the Godjam chief, was overthrown and captured.* Oobye entered into encouraging correspondence with Gosho while in arms against Kassa:

* Birro Gosho of Godjam was released from Magdāla, by the British troops, as were the two sons of Oobye of Tigre. Oobye himself died in 1867.

the latter intercepted the letters, and as soon as Gosho was subdued, and he had thereby obtained possession of all the country south and west of the Tacazze, he turned his arms against Oobye. Victory still followed his banner, and in the battle of Deraskié, fought in February 1855, the governor of Tigre, his most formidable antagonist, was overthrown. In March of the same year he took the title of Theodore III., and caused himself to be crowned by the Abuna King of Ethiopia. He, at this time, put a stop to many cruel and barbarous customs, and abolished the slave trade.

The coronation of Theodore by the Abuna led to the expulsion of the Catholic missionaries from central Abyssinia. Theodore had entered into negotiations with Padre Jacobis, who would have crowned him Emperor on consenting to adopt, for himself and the country, the Catholic faith. When Oobye was overthrown, the Abuna made some difficulty about crowning Theodore, who threatened to carry out the proposal of Padre Jacobis. The Abuna could not afford to allow the perversion of so important a proselyte. His scruples were immediately overcome. Theodore and his subjects adhered to the Coptic Church, and the Catholics, with Father Jacobis, had to seek a refuge with the rebels in the northern districts.

Theodore was now in the zenith of his career, when a misfortune fell upon him, which graved a deep impress on his subsequent life. His queen died. She had been his good genius, his counsellor, and his companion.

As soon as he was in possession of all Abyssinia, Theodore united all the forces he could command and marched against the Mohammedan Gallas, who had destroyed some churches. He obtained possession of Magdála, ravaged the Galla country, and enlisted many of the chiefs and their followers in his own ranks. He shortly afterwards reduced the outlying kingdom of Shoa; but rebellion began to make way in his annexed but not consolidated acquisitions. Disturbances broke out near Gondar and in Tigre. Owing to one of these, Mr. Plowden, who was ordered by his Government, at the beginning of 1860, to return to Massowah, while crossing the river Kaha, close to Gondar, was attacked by 400 men, headed by a rebel named Garred, received a mortal wound in the chest, and was taken prisoner. This Garred was a cousin of Theodore's, but was at the time under the command of the rebel chief Dedjatch Negussye. The merchants of Gondar paid a large ransom for Plowden. He was released, but lived only a few days. Theodore repaid the merchants, defeated Garred, and in the action the murderer of Mr. Plowden was slain by Bell, but the latter also lost his life in preserving Theodore's. Theodore avenged the deaths of both the Englishmen severely, by the slaughter or mutilation of about two thousand rebels.

In January 1861 Dedjatch Negussye fell into Theodore's hands. This chief, who was a grandson of Oobye of Tigre, had overrun all Tigre, and harassed the country as far as Gondar. The Catholic missionaries, expelled from the south by the Abuna, had obtained an asylum with him. Padre de Jacobis had settled at Halai, at the top of the Taranta pass, which leads from the Abyssinian plateau to Massowah, where he had died in 1860. The Government of the Emperor of the French had acknowledged Negussye as King of Abyssinia, and had sent a mission to him. He in return had ceded to France Annesley Bay and the island of Dissee: but the French officer who came to ratify the agreement arrived when Negussye was failing before the power of Theodore, and with difficulty escaped being taken prisoner by the chief of Dixan. The French acquisition of Annesley Bay fell to the ground. From this time cruelty seems to have formed a part of the Emperor's character. The hands and feet of Negussye were cut off, and he lingered for days in torture, without being allowed a drop of water to slack his burning thirst.

French connection with Abyssinia.

About the same date, Theodore married Terunesh, the daughter of Oobye of Tigre, who bestowed her hand upon him for her father's sake, but in her heart despised the upstart who had overthrown her own ancient family. This queen was the mother of Alamayo, who was brought to England after the death of Theodore. She herself died in the British camp on the homeward march, and was buried at Chelicut.

Theodore's union with Terunesh was not happy. He quickly tired of her and sent her with her infant son Alamayo to Magdāla. He then devoted himself to mistresses and intoxication.

<small>Captain Cameron.</small> When the news of Mr. Plowden's death reached England, Captain Cameron was appointed Consul in Abyssinia. He was detained in London some time after his appointment, in order to have a personal interview with Mr. Stern, who returned at this time from Africa. In February 1862, Captain Cameron arrived at Massowah, and in July of the same year at Gondar. By the direction of Lord Russell, Captain Cameron presented to Theodore a rifle and a pair of revolver pistols as presents from the Queen. He was received with great honour, and treated with every respect. When he arrived at Gondar a large number of Europeans were around Theodore. Six German workmen, who had been sent out as Scripture-readers, were settled at Gaffat, near Debra Tabor. These were —Flad, Waldemaier, Saalmüller, Kenzlin, Mayer, and Bender. Flad had with him his European wife, Waldemaier and Saalmüller had married daughters of Mr. Bell by an Abyssinian lady—Bender and Kenzlin were married to two daughters of Schimper, a German botanist, who had been a long time in the country, and was then at Theodore's camp. These Scripture-

readers were permitted to devote but little time to missionary labour. Theodore employed them continually in the manufacture of munitions of war and improvement of roads. There were also three missionaries in Abyssinia—Rosenthal, Brandies, and Staiger, of whom Rosenthal had an European wife. These were soon rejoined by Mr. and Mrs. Stern, who returned from Europe after Captain Cameron. The mission to which Mr. Stern belonged was established at Djenda in Dembea. There were also some adventurers around Theodore's camp—three Frenchmen, Bardel, Bourgaud, and Makerer. The second was an armourer, the last a discharged soldier; a Pole named Hall, and two German *chasseurs* who had gone to Massowah with the Duke of Saxe Coburg in 1862, and had remained in Africa to collect birds. Many of the Europeans had married Abyssinian or Galla wives, and there was accordingly quite an European colony at Gaffat.

In October 1862, Captain Cameron was dismissed by King Theodore, who sent by him a letter to the Queen of England. From Adowa, Captain Cameron forwarded this letter to Aden, whence it was despatched to England, and reached the Foreign Office on February 12, 1863. This letter, when translated, ran as follows : *

* Correspondence respecting Abyssinia laid before Parliament.

King Theodore to Her Majesty the Queen.
(Received February 12, 1863.)*

[Translation.]

IN the Name of the Father, of the Son, and of the Holy Ghost, one God in Trinity, chosen by God, King of Kings, Theodoros of Ethiopia, to Her Majesty Victoria, Queen of England. I hope your Majesty is in good health. By the power of God I am well. My fathers the Emperors having forgotten our Creator, He handed over their kingdom to the Gallas and Turks. But God created me, lifted me out of the dust, and restored this Empire to my rule. He endowed me with power, and enabled me to stand in the place of my fathers. By his power I drove away the Gallas. But for the Turks, I have told them to leave the land of my ancestors. They refuse. I am now going to wrestle with them. Mr. Plowden, and my late Grand Chamberlain, the Englishman Bell, used to tell me that there is a great Christian Queen, who loves all Christians. When they said to me this, 'We are able to make you known to her, and to establish friendship between you,' then in those times I was very glad. I gave them my love, thinking that I had found your Majesty's good-will. All men are subject to death, and my enemies, thinking to injure me, killed these my friends. But by the power of God I have exterminated those enemies, not leaving one alive, though they were of my own family, that I may get, by the power of God, your friendship.

I was prevented by the Turks occupying the sea-coast from sending you an Embassy when I was in difficulty. Consul Cameron arrived with a letter and presents of friendship. By the power of God I was very glad hearing of your welfare, and being assured of your amity. I have received your presents, and thank you much.

* Laid before Parliament, 1866.

I fear that if I send Ambassadors with presents of amity by Consul Cameron, they may be arrested by the Turks.

And now I wish that you may arrange for the safe passage of my Ambassadors everywhere on the road.

I wish to have an answer to this letter by Consul Cameron, and that he may conduct my Embassy to England. See how the Islam oppress the Christian!

After forwarding this letter, Captain Cameron proceeded to Bogos, a small province at the extreme north-east of Abyssinia, nearly surrounded by Egyptian territory. The Christians of Bogos had been plundered by the Shangallas, black tribes under the dominion of Egypt, and Captain Cameron, in imitation of the conduct of Consul Plowden under similar circumstances, went to Bogos, to do what he could in behalf of the Christian community. In this journey, he was accompanied by Samuel, afterwards known as Samuel the King's steward. From Bogos, where he left Samuel, he proceeded to Kassala, the centre of the Egyptian administration in that quarter. At Kassala, he met Mr. Speedy, whom he sent as vice-consul to Massowah, while he remained away from that port. Thence he travelled to Matamma. Here he was taken ill, and, in order to recruit his health in a cool climate, returned to the highland of Abyssinia, and reached Djenda in August 1863. Captain Cameron's visit to Egyptian territory had been dictated purely by a desire of affording protection to oppressed Christians, and for the purpose of collecting information with regard to the slave trade in the Soudan.

At the same time as Captain Cameron received Theodore's letter for the Queen of England, a letter was despatched to the Emperor of the French by the Negoos. Of this M. Bardel was the bearer. He was not received well by the Court of Tuilleries, and returned to Theodore with loud complaints against the Emperor of the French. During his absence, M. Lejean, a French gentleman who had been appointed consul at Massowah, visited Theodore's court. He was accompanied by a physician named Dr. Legard and by Mr. Dufton.* At his audience with Theodore, he presented a letter from the French Minister of Foreign Affairs, as well as some valuable presents.

Imprisonment of French Consul by Theodore. At the time of the arrival of M. Lejean, Theodore was on the point of setting out on an incursion into the province of Godjam, which had revolted. M. Lejean accompanied him in this expedition, which set out on February 11. At the beginning of March, the Frenchman, weary with Abyssinian life and the hardships of the campaign, resolved to demand his dismissal. Theodore refused to see him. M. Lejean attempted to force his way into the Emperor's presence, who put him in irons for four-and-twenty hours. He was then released, and sent to Gaffat. On the

* Mr. Dufton towards the close of the expedition was murdered by a party of Shohos in the Senafe Pass.

return of Bardel, Theodore considered that he had been insulted by the Emperor of the French, and ordered his representative to immediately quit Abyssinia. M. Lejean set out from Gondar on October 2, 1863. It was thus a French subject who was the first European that suffered under Theodore, and in whose person the law of nations and the sacred character of ambassador were violated by the Negoos.

In October Mr. Stern obtained leave to return to the coast. On his way he passed the King's camp in Woggera, and stopped to pay his respects. He was seized and imprisoned. On November 13, a detachment of troops was sent to Djenda, seized most of the missionaries as well as Mrs. Flad, brought them to the King's camp, and loaded them with chains. On November 20 a public court was held, at which Mr. Stern and Mr. Rosenthal were tried. Many charges of a puerile nature were brought against them; and the Europeans were assembled to be their judges. The prisoners were, after the trial, kept in close confinement.

Almost immediately after this, on November 22, a young Irishman, Kerans, who had come out to act as secretary to Captain Cameron, arrived at Gondar. He was the bearer of despatches from the Foreign Office to Captain Cameron, in one of which the latter was ordered to quit Abyssinia and return to Massowah. There was no answer to Theodore's letter to the Queen. Theodore was enraged.

Captain Cameron, after the arrival of Kerans, was summoned to the King's camp, and told to remain there until further orders. He wished to return to Gondar on the plea of bad health, but was not allowed to do so. On December 4, Stern and Rosenthal were summoned before the Negoos. The knives were prepared to cut off their hands and feet. They were only saved from horrible mutilation and a lingering death by the intercession of the Abuna.

Till the beginning of January Consul Cameron waited, when he informed the Emperor that he was ordered to Massowah, and requested permission to be allowed to leave in a few days.

Imprisonment of Captain Cameron.

On the following morning, January 4, 1864, Captain Cameron, his European servants, the Gondar missionaries, and Mr. Stern and Mr. Rosenthal, were summoned into Theodore's presence. Captain Cameron was rudely interrogated as to there being no letter to Theodore sent by Mr. Kerans from Queen Victoria; and the Negoos abruptly closed the interview by ordering them all to be kept close prisoners. M. Bardel was then sent off to Kassala, probably for the purpose of finding out what an Egyptian general with a considerable force was doing at Matamma; of investigating what Captain Cameron had been doing during his journey in that quarter; as well as to enquire into a Quixotish enterprise undertaken by some Frenchmen, under Comte de Bisson, against Abyssinia. Bisson's expedition never reached Abyssinian territory, but failed at Barea, where Bisson began to fortify the permanent camp, when he was immediately brought back to Kassala by a strong detachment of Egyptian troops. It disquieted Theodore, however, who no doubt thought that Captain Cameron's visit to Kassala in the previous year had some connection with Bisson's enterprise. On the return of Bardel, the European workmen from Gaffat were summoned by the Negoos to deliberate in a special council on the liberation of the captives. On February 4 the council was held, and, by the recommendation of the Gaffat Scripture-readers, Flad, Staiger, Brandies, Cornelius,* and the two German chasseurs, were set at liberty. The British Consul, his suite, Mr. Stern and Mr. Rosenthal, were kept in chains. The head of the Gaffat missionaries told Captain Cameron that he would request Theodore to release him and the other prisoners if Cameron would engage that England would insist on no satisfaction for the insult offered to her Envoy. This Captain Cameron declined to undertake. He and his companions were retained in captivity.†

A few days afterwards M. Bardel was himself added to the number of captives, when Theodore found his services no longer requisite.

* Cornelius died before the release of the other Europeans.
† Dr. Blanc's *Captivity in Abyssinia*.

On February 14 the Scripture-readers were ordered back to Gaffat, and the prisoners who had been liberated were sent there also to work with them in the manufacture of matériel of war. On the same day Captain Cameron contrived to send a note in pencil to Mr. Speedy at Massowah, in which he told that he himself, his suite—consisting of Kerans, McKelvie, and Pietro—as well as Stern, Rosenthal, and Makerer, were confined in chains at Gondar, and that their release was hopeless until the receipt of a civil letter in answer to that of Theodore to the Queen.

<small>Torture of Mr. Stern.</small> On May 12 the captives, and especially Mr. Stern, were most brutally tortured. The torture was repeated again on the night of the 13th. The particulars of the atrocious sufferings to which they were subjected by the command of the Negoos have been already told by Mr. Stern. After the rains of 1864 Theodore started for a campaign in Godjam against the rebel Tadela Guralu, and the captives were sent off to Amba Magdāla chained two-and-two together. In Magdāla they were detained in hand-chains till July 1, 1865, when Menilek, the Crown Prince of Shoa, who had also been a prisoner in the fortress, escaped. Theodore, who watched him with a glass, saw him received by a number of Gallas, and was thereat so incensed that he ordered the execution of all the Mohammedan Galla prisoners, among others, of the son of the Galla queen, Werkait, who was in his hands as a hostage. These unfortunates had their hands and feet hacked off, and

then their mutilated and bleeding but still living carcasses were hurled over the precipitous rock on which the amba stood. Hand-chains as well as ancle-chains were also placed on the Christian prisoners, and the two were fastened together so that the wearers were bent double, and thus rendered unable to stand erect by day or stretch their wearied limbs at night. Thus they remained till February 25, 1866, when they heard of the arrival of Mr. Rassam at the camp of the Negoos, and were ordered to be set at liberty.

When the news of Consul Cameron's detention in Abyssinia arrived in England it was hardly believed. It was soon, however, proved true by the receipt of his letter. The Foreign Office selected Mr. Hormuzd Rassam, Assistant Political Resident at Aden, to be the bearer of a letter from the Queen of England to Theodore. Mr. Rassam was also furnished with a letter from the Coptic Patriarch of Alexandria to Theodore, and one from the same spiritual chief to the Abuna. The Queen's letter was translated into Arabic in Egypt, and forwarded to Mr. Rassam at Aden, whence he set out on July 20, 1864, for Massowah, in H.M.S. 'Dalhousie,' accompanied by Dr. Blanc. On the 23rd Mr. Rassam arrived at Massowah, and on the following day sent off messengers to Theodore with the letters from the Patriarch to the Abuna and the Emperor, as well as with one from himself to Theodore, announcing the arrival of the Queen's letter at

Mission of Mr. Rassam.

Massowah. Mr. Rassam also informed the Negoos that he was desirous of delivering the Queen's letter in person; that at Massowah he would await the Emperor's reply, and that in case the Emperor desired his presence, he solicited to be provided with an escort. For a long time Mr. Rassam received no answer, but he was enabled to communicate with the captives, and to supply them with stores and money. In February 1865, as no answer was received from Theodore, it was thought that perhaps Mr. Rassam's mission would acquire more dignity by the addition of a military officer. Lieutenant Prideaux of the Bombay Staff Corps was therefore attached to it. He arrived at Massowah in May of the same year. As no intelligence could be obtained from Theodore, a letter was again sent by a relation of Samuel, the Emperor's steward, who happened to be at Massowah. He returned, after a long lapse of time, in July, with information that Captain Cameron was released, and brought with him a letter from Theodore, neither signed nor sealed, in which he ordered Mr. Rassam and his companions to proceed to Matamma, and inform him of their arrival at that place. In the meantime the Government had ordered Mr. Rassam to withdraw, and had appointed in his stead Mr. Palgrave, the celebrated traveller in Arabia. Mr. Rassam under these circumstances considered it his duty to go to Egypt, and request further orders. He telegraphed the news of Captain Cameron's release home; when he arrived in Egypt on September 5. Here Mr. Palgrave was ordered to remain, and Mr. Rassam ordered to return to Massowah. He arrived there on September 25, where he found that letters had arrived from the captives in which a denial of their release was made, and that on the contrary they had had hand-chains added to their previous bonds. These letters had been taken to Aden by a man-of-war. Mr. Rassam, in order to make himself acquainted with their contents, and to consult with the Political Resident at that station, Colonel Merewether, went to Aden. Captain Cameron's letter, which had arrived there, contained an earnest appeal to Mr. Rassam* to go up to Theodore at once, as his declining to do so would prove of the utmost danger to the prisoners. Colonel Merewether accordingly advised Mr. Rassam to proceed.

Mr. Rassam, Dr. Blanc, and Lieutenant Prideaux returned to the African coast. On October 15 they left Massowah, and arrived at Kassala on November 6; on the 17th at Sheik Abu Sin, capital of the province of Kedaref, and at Matamma on November 21. They thus, deducting seven days when they were forced to halt for want of carriage, accomplished the distance of five hundred and forty miles in thirty days. Their track had lain through the unhealthy lowland of the Soudan, which teems with fever and malaria. They

* Dr. Blanc's *Captivity in Abyssinia.*

had travelled with all speed, but at the expiration of much time and trouble were only within the same distance of Magdāla as they would have been in Annesley Bay.*

The day after his arrival at Matamma Mr. Rassam despatched two messengers to Theodore to inform him of his arrival. After a month's delay these returned with courteous messages; on December 25 (1865), Sheik Jumna, the governor of Matamma, who paid tribute to both the Negoos and the Viceroy, was ordered to treat the mission well, and to provide them with camels as far as Wochnee, where they would be met by an Abyssinian escort.

On December 28, the party left Matamma, crossed into Abyssinia, and on the 30th arrived at Wochnee.

On January 25, Mr. Rassam's mission arrived at Theodore's camp in Damot. They were received with all honour, and delivered the Queen's letter. Theodore signified his intention of releasing the prisoners, and himself accompanied them a part of the way to Kourata or Lake Tsana, which was to be their residence until the arrival of the captives from Magdāla. At Kourata the mission was attended by Samuel the King's steward who acted as valderaba (introducer), and also, on account of his knowledge of Arabic, had been inter-

* These remarks are necessary, as some people who have little knowledge of the subject have advocated the unhealthy route through the Soudan as the one by which the British forces should have advanced to assail Magdāla.

preter between Theodore and Mr. Rassam. On February 17, the party arrived at Kourata, where a few days afterwards it was joined by the Gaffat people, who had been ordered by Theodore to come to Kourata, in case the mission might feel lonely.

On March 12, the captives from Magdāla, who were joined at Debra Tabor by those there, arrived at Kourata. Theodore was at this time engaged in plundering and destroying with fire the crops, villages, and towns in Damot, Metcha, and Zagé. He sent, however, some charges, which were read to the captives, and these, after acknowledging that they had done wrong, were to be released. A few days later, Theodore wrote to Mr. Rassam, requesting him to write for workmen, and to await their return. Mr. Rassam, in return, said it would be better if he was allowed to depart, as he could better represent the desires of his Majesty. Theodore then sent a courteous invitation to Mr. Rassam to spend a day with him, and on March 25, received him at the town of Zagé.

Theodore met Mr. Rassam and his companions with every token of deference. His object was to obtain European workmen, and he attempted to accomplish his purpose with cringing servility. In private, he was, however, very much annoyed that Mr. Rassam had not written for the artisans, and he took counsel of his own chiefs and the Gaffat people whether he should let the Europeans go. He was counselled by all to permit the Europeans to depart. Mr. Rassam and his companions returned to Kourata, in the expectation of immediately setting out with their released countrymen for England. They were destined to be grievously disappointed.

<small>Imprisonment of Mr. Rassam.</small>

On April 13, the Magdála and Gaffat prisoners started for the coast. Mr. Rassam's mission, accompanied by the Gaffat workpeople, were to pay a visit to King Theodore, and afterwards to meet the prisoners at Tankal near the north-west extremity of Lake Tsana, whence all were to start for Massowah together. At Zagé, Mr. Rassam was met by Ras Engeddah,[*] Theodore's prime-minister, and treated with every respect. He was conducted into the tent of the Negoos, where the Abyssinian grandees were collected. The throne was also there, but Theodore was absent. At a given signal, soldiers rushed on Mr. Rassam and his companions, tore off their accoutrements, submitted them to great indignity, and made them prisoners. The prisoners who had departed on the Tankal road were also brought back and confined. The excuse advanced by Theodore for this conduct was that the prisoners had been sent away without being reconciled to him. On April 17, all the Europeans were brought before Theodore, who dictated a letter to the Queen of England, of which Mr. Flad was to be the bearer. Mr. Flad was also the bearer of a letter from Mr.

[*] Ras Engeddah was afterwards killed in the assault on Magdála.

Rassam to Lord Clarendon, the then Secretary of State for Foreign Affairs, which was written by the order of and inspected by Theodore. In both of these letters application was made for European workmen, and machinery for the manufacture of munitions of war, and for an instructor of artillery. Mr. Flad left the camp April 21, arrived in Alexandria June 29, and in London July 10.

The detention of Mr. Rassam as a means to obtain artillery was probably not unconnected with the fact that Theodore's power was already waning. His large army had depopulated whole provinces which were hostile to him, but now he was compelled to devastate provinces even friendly to him, as insurrection and rebellion were closing upon him. Gobaze, the descendant of the royal house of Zague, whose father had been hanged by Theodore, raised the standard of revolt in 1865, in Lasta. He was quickly joined by the mountaineers of that district, by large numbers of discontented peasantry, and was aided by the soldiery of his stepfather, the chief of Wadela. All Lasta succumbed to him. He then marched against Tigre, where he defeated Theodore's general, and left as ruler his lieutenant, Dedjatch Kassai. Wadela, Enderta, Dalanta, and Damot afterwards submitted to him. In 1865, Menilek, Prince of Shoa, escaped from Magdāla, and called his retainers together against Theodore. The Gallas were also in constant enmity with the Negoos.

Declension of Theodore's power.

Till the end of June, the Europeans, although detained as prisoners, were not unkindly treated. They were then sent to Magdála, where they were soon afterwards put in chains. They suffered hunger, cold, and misery, till the spring of 1868; and in constant fear of any angry paroxysm of the Negoos faced the bitterness of death, till they were relieved by the British troops.

In December 1866, they heard that Mr. Flad had reached Massowah, bringing with him a letter from the Queen to Theodore. In this letter Her Majesty said that machinery had been sent to Massowah, to be handed over to Theodore's officers who should bring down the captives to that place. Some artisans also accompanied Mr. Flad. Colonel Merewether arrived at Massowah at the same time, and wrote to Theodore that he would only allow the artisans to proceed into Abyssinia when the captives were returned to him. These letters had no effect on Theodore. For many weary months the prisoners lingered on. It was not till December 1867 that they heard that British troops had landed in the country of their captivity, and were marching to their release.

From the time that Mr. Rassam and his companions left Theodore for Magdála, his cruelties and atrocities increased. He shortly afterwards plundered Gondar, pillaged the churches, burnt the buildings, and had many priests and young girls cast alive into the flames.

In April 1867, the rebellion brought about by his misdeeds was almost general against Theodore. Except his fortresses and his camp little of his acquisitions owned his authority. In April 1867, fearful that his European workmen at Gaffat might be seized by some rebel, he moved them into his camp. At the same time he began the construction of two roads from Debra Tabor, one towards Godjam, the other towards Magdāla. At this time the Gaffat people, in order to court Theodore's favour, and, if possible, to avert from themselves the executions, floggings, and beatings which were continually being carried on, proposed to cast for him a gigantic mortar. The idea delighted him: the work was commenced, and was not without influence on the British Expedition.

In the spring of 1867, Dedjatch Kassai, the lieutenant of Wagshum Gobaze in Tigre, rebelled against his master, and assumed the supreme power of that province.

On April 26, 1867, Mr. Flad found Theodore in Dembea. His army was rapidly deserting him. He could hardly obtain food for his followers. The peasantry destroyed their own crops and villages at the sign of his approach, but revenged themselves on the Negoos by cutting off his stragglers and nightly alarming his camp. He retorted by torturing and executing all who fell into his hands. In one month, in Begemder, he killed or burnt alive more than

3,000 people. Famine now threatened his camp, which became almost uninhabitable by the smell of horses and mules which had died from starvation.

Theodore moves to Magdála. Under these circumstances, Theodore resolved to quit Debra Tabor and march to Magdála. Waggons to convey his artillery were prepared. On October 10, 1867, he set out, having first burnt Debra Tabor. His march was difficult and harassed. By desertions, death, and his own executions, his army was reduced to about 5,000 men. On the line of march his troops were surrounded by peasantry and rebels, who cut off every straggler and missed no chance of plunder. Every day the road must be made for the passage of the artillery. The distances daily traversed were necessarily short. On November 22, he reached the steep acclivity which leads from the plain of Begemder up to the plateau of Zebit. He had to quarry a road up the basalt precipice which forms the face of this ascent. By December 15 this road was ready, and on the 25th he encamped on the Wadela plateau, above the ravine of the Jidda. Here arduous work awaited him. The descent to the Jidda and ascent on the Dalanta side are nearly precipitous. Up and down these the road had to be carried, and the heavy ordnance dragged. Theodore made friends with the peasantry of Dalanta, and employed large working parties of the country people as well as his own soldiers to push on the road. On January 10 he began his descent, and reached the bottom of the ravine on the 28th. Thence he gradually ascended and encamped on the plateau of Dalanta on February 20, within sight of the fortress of Magdāla.

Meanwhile, the British captives within that prison-house wore away a monotonous existence of misery and squalor, unbroken except by frequent fright and constant terror of torture and of death.

CHAPTER II.

PREPARATION OF EXPEDITION.

Origin of expedition.

YET the captives in the hands of Theodore had not been forgotten by the people of England. Frequent appeals in their behalf had been made to the Government. Several travellers had volunteered to attempt their liberation. But the statesmen who guided the actions of the country were unwilling to risk more envoys in the hands of a barbarian chieftain who paid no respect to the office of ambassador. The rulers of England, supported by the public opinion of the country, were loth to thrust an expedition into a distant land, shrouded in mystery, where danger alone was certain. The disasters of the Crimea still hung heavy on men's minds. An idea was widely spread abroad not only in this country, but throughout Europe, that through some adverse disposition of the British character it was impossible but that England should fail in any military enterprise which depended more on the spirit of order than on the stubborn courage of her troops. Men in India, confident in the power shown in the suppression of the great mutiny, thought otherwise. Accustomed to treat with a high hand restive princes of the more civilised East, who so much as lifted a voice against the English name, they writhed beneath the insult which a British envoy had received at the hands of an African savage. They loudly spoke out their opinions. These were carried home and acted as a stimulus on the minority of public opinion, which did not yet despair of the prowess of the country. The tiny band which had always advocated the rescue of the captives by force, gained in numbers and brought its weight to bear upon the Government. Colonel Merewether, the Political Resident at Aden, perpetually urged upon the notice of the Foreign Office that force alone would ever cause Theodore to yield up his prisoners. He dwelt strongly in his despatches upon this point. Had it not been for Merewether, the captives might yet linger in chains at Magdála. He was the author of the Abyssinian Expedition. Of high courage and chivalrous temperament, Merewether chided the delay in the employment of troops. He clearly foresaw and predicted that no diplomacy would suffice, and that embassies would only deliver more prisoners into the hands of Theodore. His representations were not without effect. It appears that towards the middle of April 1867, the Government first began to contemplate the possibility of an expedition to Abyssinia. Those who understood the matter and had hitherto deprecated an incursion of British troops into a land known only to be rugged and barren, in the spring of this year had reluctantly come to the conclusion that no other measures would avail for the rescue of Mr. Rassam and his companions in captivity. Among those whose opinions were now altered was Sir William Coghlan. To his counsels Ministers listened attentively. It was, however, only reluctantly and dubiously that the Government determined upon sending an expedition. With the view of such an eventual necessity, in April, the Secretary of State for Foreign Affairs, in whose department the management of the Abyssinian difficulty had hitherto lain, officially invited the attention of the Secretary of War and of the Secretary for India to the subject. In June, the Government sought information as to the possibility of an expedition into the country of Theodore.

Choice of base of operations.

As soon as the idea of a possible invasion of Abyssinia was conceived by the Ministers of England, it was natural that they should look around to see whence a force could most conveniently be thrown upon the eastern coast of Africa. An army could have been prepared in England and sent by way of Egypt to Abyssinia. Many thought that this course should have been adopted. But such an army could only have been organised and equipped on Egyptian territory, or on the sea-shore of Africa. It would have been composed of troops not yet inured to a tropical climate, and could have depended for its supplies, &c. from England alone. Double marine transport would have been required, as the combatants and their supplies must have been carried in vessels from England to Alexandria. Across Egypt they could have been transported only slowly by railway. The transport of the stores across the isthmus of Suez would have been very expensive, even if the canal had been made use of. A separate fleet of shipping would again have been required to carry the soldiery and materials of war down the Red Sea. The constant changes would have been not only inconvenient, but would have sacrificed to no purpose both time and money. Aden is the nearest point to Massowah, over which the British flag floats. The scarcity of water on that arid, volcanic rock, and the small space included within the British boundary, made Aden unsuitable for the preparation and organisation of an expeditionary army. The directors of the possible invasion must therefore look farther off. On the western shore of Hindostan are two great harbours— Kurrachee and Bombay. The former, the gateway of Sind, the key of the traffic of the Indus, has not, however, the same advantages as the base of an expedition as her more southern sister. Bombay is the merchant queen of the eastern seas, the portal of the rapid commerce of Hindostan, the first naval station of British India. In her harbour floats the craft of all nations. Her storehouses teem with the products of every quarter of the globe. In the Presidency of Bombay is quartered the least prejudiced and not the least faithful portion of the Indian army of Britain. The sepoys of Bombay object less to cross the ocean than do those of Bengal or Madras. Their caste is less tenacious of its rites and diet. They had already proved high capability of foreign service in the Persian war. Affghanistan, Sind, Beloochistan, Central India, and the Punjab had borne testimony to their prowess in the field. British troops also could conveniently be drawn from the interior and assembled at the port. Bombay was eminently fitted to be the starting-point of the enterprise. At this time the Governor of Bombay was Mr. Seymour Fitzgerald—a politician of no slight fame in the debates of Parliament and in the Government in England. On the accession of Lord Derby's Ministry to power, he had been entrusted with the presidential administration of Bombay. Mr. Fitzgerald, although eminent as a politician, had as yet had little experience of military rule. In India, where empire is maintained by the sword, he had indeed acquired some military experience, but in many things was dependent on his advisers. Schooled to study popular feeling, he was most careful of the financial prosperity of the district over which he ruled; and from an eager and well-intentioned economy, sometimes failed to perceive that a large expenditure at the beginning may in some enterprises be the surest preven-

CHAP. II.] PREPARATION OF EXPEDITION. 51

tive of lavish waste in the issue. At his call, Sir Robert Napier, the Commander-in-Chief of the Bombay army, was prompt to tender military advice. But Mr. Fitzgerald relied more upon other counsellors.

The Ministry of England judged that in the event of an invasion of Abyssinia, Bombay must be the base of operations. On July 10, the Secretary of State for India telegraphed to the Governor of that Presidency, the demand how soon, *if an expedition were determined upon*, the force could be ready to start from Bombay fully equipped and provisioned. No orders were given for preparation. Information alone was required with the view to an only possible contingency. Yet this telegram was not unimportant: it pointed out to the Government of Bombay that its Presidency would be adopted for the base of operations against Abyssinia.

Mr. Fitzgerald, on the receipt of this important telegram from the Government at home, conferred with Sir Robert Napier. The latter was unaware that it might be his own fortune to command the expedition, for which thought alone was now taken. He was asked only for counsel; and under the belief that some other would be called to the supreme guidance, he gave his advice for the composition of the army which afterwards handled by himself achieved so much.

At this time Colonel Phayre was Quartermaster-General of the Bombay army; a man of tall and

Compilation of information.

powerful figure, of iron constitution, and indefatigable in labour, he was well suited for an office which requires in its possessor a superfluity of both physical and mental exertion. Sir Robert Napier, the Commander-in-Chief at Bombay, caused all available sources of information to be searched for a knowledge of the nature of the country. All the books and records that the library of the Bombay Asiatic Society and the archives of the Government could supply were placed in the hands of the Quartermaster-General. Colonel Phayre waded through a vast mass of travels and correspondence, and condensed the result of his investigations in a brief report. From this information it appeared that Massowah, or its neighbourhood, would be the point most convenient for the disembarkation of an expedition to obtain the release of the European captives imprisoned at Magdāla. It seemed that the best route for the army to pursue would be found in the most direct line to the latter place. This line would lead by way of Antalo and Lake Ashangi, and would cut almost at right angles the lines of general watershed of the country; as it would, however, cut the streams near their sources, they would not be such formidable obstacles as the large rivers which must be encountered in an advance by way of Matamna and Kassala. On such meagre information had Sir Robert Napier to form his dispositions.* He recommended

---

* Memorandum of Sir Robert Napier, July 23, 1867.

that an advanced force should be despatched as early as possible to make arrangements for the formation of a base of operations in the vicinity of Massowah, as well as for the convenience and protection of the troops and stores on first landing. The distance between Massowah and Magdāla was computed at about 400 miles ; Antalo, the capital of the province of Enderta, was believed to be a considerable place, about halfway between the coast and the fortress. Sir Robert Napier calculated, from such information as he could collate, that Theodore's cruelties had rendered most of his neighbours hostile to his dynasty, and at this early period looked forward to securing the aid of the people of Tigre and of the Gallas in the operations. Yet he did not neglect to perceive that Theodore's quarrels with his neighbours might not be permanent : that they might reconcile themselves to him and band with him against a foreign invader, or that intriguers of other nations might raise hostility in the country against the members of a British expedition. Nor did his humane and Christian feelings allow him to regard with callous indifference the prospect of British soldiers being the means of allowing the pagan Gallas to overwhelm the representatives of a corrupt and vitiated still not yet moribund Christianity : nor did he contemplate making use of some portion of the people to leave it, after the departure of the expedition, to the terrible vengeance which is dealt out to their enemies by the barbarous tribes of Africa. He did not despise the friendship of such races, nor was he averse to receiving any assistance they could afford, but he firmly held that a British expedition should be sufficiently strong to do its own work with ease and security. For this purpose he considered that a force of about 12,000 men would be required. Such a force could hold with security its base of operations near the sea, and could maintain a supporting force at a distance of about 200 miles from the coast. It could also detach an advanced party of about 5,000 men, which should act over the last 200 miles to Magdála or to such other place as the prisoners might be conveyed, and cover their communications.

Suggestions of Sir R. Napier.

Sir Robert Napier impressed upon the Government that although, by proper arrangements, meat, corn, and forage might be procured in the country, still that to render a force efficient a large quantity of carriage would be required. He advocated the employ of mules, but also of camels and carts, as well as the formation of a corps of 3,000 coolies. A Chinese cooly corps had done good service in the army of Sir Hope Grant which in 1860 reduced the Taku forts and planted the standard of St. George on the walls of Pekin. He urged that agents with sufficient funds should be despatched to the best places for procuring cattle and supplies, and that officials should also be stationed at Massowah with ample authority and means to direct the preliminary arrangements. In his correspondence it will also be found that he insisted upon the development by these officers of the local carriage of the country, which he inferred must exist on account of the salt-trade of Abyssinia. This suggestion was ultimately attended to by the officers sent forward to develop the local resources of the country, but not till after much valuable time had been wasted.

Sir Robert Napier did not fail to point out that the Government, which immediately directed the operations, should have full authority to provide everything necessary for the health and comfort of the troops. Nor did he omit to observe that no such expedition could be carried out without very great expenditure, and that the very best arrangements might be crippled by some misplaced economy. From a very imperfect meteorological register kept by Harris, he concluded that the troops would be obliged to encounter both rain and cold, and that it was absolutely necessary that the soldiers should have their tents, warm clothing, and a waterproof sheet for each man.

On July 23, Sir Robert Napier submitted officially the above views to the Government of Bombay. He had previously* demi-officially answered Mr. Fitzgerald's

---

* Sir R. Napier's letter to Mr. Fitzgerald, July 13.
Force, 3 regiments of European infantry.
      7 ,,   Native ,,
      4 ,,   Cavalry.
4 batteries of field artillery.
Punjab pioneers.

queries as to how soon a force such as that which the Government proposed could be ready for service in Abyssinia. Before writing this letter he consulted with the officers of the army departments, and came to the conclusion that in everything, except carriage, such a force could be equipped in from three to four months. Not much carriage could be collected at Bombay, and transplanted so as to be immediately ready to move. Sir Robert Napier suggested that attention should be turned to Aden, Egypt, and Abyssinia itself; that carriage should be collected as near the point of debarkation as possible, and that every exertion should be made to enlist and develop the native carriage of the country. He considered that the advanced party could not commence its enquiries too soon, and should have an escort to enable it to reconnoitre freely; and that troops should be obtained from Madras and Bengal to relieve troops sent from Bombay to Abyssinia. He held that mountain artillery ought to be attached to the expedition, but urged Mr. Fitzgerald to impress on the Home Government the necessity of giving early orders for carriage and commissariat.

On July 25, the Home Government telegraphed for further information, with a view to an expedition, in case one might be decided upon. Orders were also received at Bombay directing that a reconnoitring party of such officers as Sir Robert Napier might advise to be necessary, should be sent to the Abyssinian coast, to make enquiries on the spot, and to communicate with Colonel Merewether, the Political Resident at Aden. Sir Robert Napier, by his memorandum of July 23, had anticipated the demand for further information. He now urged the immediate despatch of the reconnoitring party. Mr. Fitzgerald considered it advisable to await the information brought by Colonel Merewether, who was ordered to Bombay from Aden.

On the last day of July, Sir Stafford Northcote, the Secretary of State for India, telegraphed to the Governor of Bombay to begin the collection of transport animals. This order was repeated on August 1, accompanied with a telegraphic demand as to what would be required from England. But not yet had the Cabinet fully decided on prosecuting the campaign, and till it was finally determined what would be the issue of the ministerial consultations in London, the preparations at Bombay were naturally crippled and lukewarm. By August 13, the Cabinet had decided upon the despatch of a force to Africa, and the Secretary of State for India telegraphed to Bombay that it was proposed that Sir Robert Napier should be the Commander-in-Chief of the Expedition to Abyssinia. Rightly England made her choice: he had been well trained in campaigns and political duties in India.

In the middle of August the Duke of Cambridge

Collection of transport.

recommended that Sir Robert Napier should be the Commander-in-Chief of the Abyssinian Expedition. In former wars English statesmen have been apt to interfere with the generals commanding English armies, and have striven from the cabinet at home to direct the actions in the field. Sir Robert Napier was more fortunate. A practical soldier was at the head of the British army. His royal birth, his experience in the field, and his well-known zeal for his profession gave weight to his words. He strongly impressed upon the Government the necessity that after statesmen have made their choice of a general they should leave him unhampered by any interruptions, and content themselves with supplying his demands and requirements. In this clear-sighted course the Duke of Cambridge was worthily supported by Sir Stafford Northcote, the Secretary of State for India. As far as the Government of England was concerned, Sir Robert Napier enjoyed more advantages than usually fall to the lot of a British commander. Abroad he was not so fortunate.

As soon as the expedition was determined upon, the Field Marshal Commanding-in-Chief and the Secretary of State for War allowed Sir Robert Napier to seek his materials from the whole army both in England and India. No questions of routine or precedent were permitted to stand in his way. By these aids he was enabled to draw the officers of his staff from England as well as from India. Among those who came from the former country for the expedition were Milward, who afterwards commanded the mountain guns, and Thesiger, the Deputy Adjutant-General of the force.

The various departments of the Government assisted each to the best of its ability. As Abyssinia has no sea-board, the Foreign Office obtained permission for disembarkation on Egyptian soil. It also engaged its agencies in the Mediterranean ports to aid in the purchase of animals for the transport service of the expedition. The War Department laid open its stores and arsenals to supply the demands from Bombay. The Admiralty took measures for lighting and buoying the approaches to Massowah through the intricate and dangerous coral reefs which abound on the western margin of the Red Sea. Vessels were chartered by that department for the conveyance of animals from the ports of the Mediterranean and Levant to Alexandria. Other vessels teeming with warlike cargoes were engaged to sail from the Thames to Bombay. They carried clothing, ammunition, and breech-loading arms for the British troops who were to be thrown into the unknown region. Three large ships were despatched to act as floating hospitals in the port of debarkation. The climate of the sea-board was supposed to be almost deadly to the European constitution. Every precaution was adopted to lessen and alleviate its baneful effects.

These ships were fitted with every appliance which science could suggest or experience dictate for the restoration of the sick and the comfort of the suffering. Tried and skilled surgeons were stationed on board of them. Nor were the researches of science adapted to minister to the comfort of the sick and wounded alone. Vast stores of coal were sent to the Cape of Good Hope, Bombay, and Aden to provide the motive power for the transit of troops, and the means of condensing from the sea fresh water for the use of men and animals. The electric fluid was pressed into the use of the campaign, and a telegraph was constructed suitable for service in the field, to connect the office of the commander with the vessels of the fleet. The discoveries of chemists were combined with the skill of the mechanician to enable the outposts by means of lamps to flash instantaneously their observations to head-quarters. By another arrangement, for Theodore was reported to be daring in attacks conducted under the cover of darkness, the whole of the country adjacent to a camp could be illumined by a light as useful as the sun. The power of steam was not to be limited to the sea alone. Preparations were made for sending out a railway to connect the landing place with the interior, but these were rendered unnecessary by its being obtained from Bombay. Condensers such as the latest experiments of science had proved to be the most efficacious were supplied for use on shore. Piping of iron many miles in length was sent forth to collect the slender rills of the African mountains, and carry their waters to the stations of the British troops. Carts for the conveyance of supplies, and ambulances for the carriage of the wounded, with the harness for their draught animals, were sent forth from the storehouses of Woolwich, while the factories of Enfield hurried to supply the Europeans of the expedition with breech-loading fire-arms. Special artillery, fitted for mountain warfare, was prepared at the Royal gun factories, and equipped for transport on the backs of mules. Wells were obtained for finding water in inland positions, and powerful pumps for forcing it to the surface within the easy reach of thirsty claimants.

It was necessary that the army should be provided with treasure. Without the means of paying its way it could have obtained no supplies in the country. The natives would have withered away before its presence. No coinage was current in Abyssinia except the Maria Theresa dollar of Austria. To obtain these, British agents were employed to buy all that they could obtain in Southern Germany, and British influence set the machinery of the mint at Vienna in motion. These dollars were shipped from Trieste to Alexandria, thence conveyed to Suez, and despatched to the scene of operations. Truly, the rulers of England did well. The experience of the Russian war was not forgotten. Europe in general looked upon the undertaking with the smile of quiet scorn.

Feeling of the people of England.

To the majority of men in England the Abyssinian Expedition appeared foolish and chimerical. Arguments repeatedly appeared against it in the daily journals. Letters from correspondents were inserted in their columns, which drew ghastly pictures of the malaria of the coast and the insalubrity of the country. At times the expedition was to die of thirst, at times to be destroyed by hippopotami. Every beast antagonistic to the life of man was, according to these writers, to be found in the jungles or the swamps of that treacherous country. Animals were to perish by flies, men by worms. The return of the expedition was regarded as chimerical, the massacre of the prisoners as certain. The climate was hastily laid down as similar to that of the West Coast of Africa. Insurance offices raised their rates mercilessly to the officers volunteering for the service, who were regarded as rushing blindfold into suicide. Yet there was much curiosity manifested with regard to Abyssinia. Many were eager competitors for military service in that unknown land, and numbers of applicants besieged the press to be allowed to act as special correspondents. Men of science were attached to the army. Foreign officers were also, at the wish of their governments, permitted to accompany head-quarters. The Government pursued its course not without hope that Theodore, terrified by the menace of an invasion, might yield.

At Bombay men were not idle while preparation was being made in England. As soon as the intelligence that the expedition was to proceed reached Bombay, on August 18, the din of preparation and hum of bustle began steadily to rise from her arsenals and dockyards. The wish of the Government of England was, without doubt, to leave all arrangements entirely to the Commander-in-Chief of the Bombay army.* This unfortunately was not made sufficiently explicit. The local government of the Presidency did not allow the interference of the supreme government of India in any of its arrangements, yet it did not accord a perfect compliance to the wishes of the nominated commander of the expedition. Hence arose some inconvenience.

One of the first points towards which attention was turned, was the organisation of the force to be employed. This was naturally dependent upon the plan of the campaign, which must be of an elastic nature, so as to meet all the possible contingencies of its unknown theatre. Sir Robert Napier, conscious that over such a long line of communication as lay between the sea-coast and Magdāla, many detached posts would be necessary, strongly advocated the employment of several regiments weak in numbers

* Despatch of India Office, September 30.

rather than of one or two of great strength. He also perceived the necessity of wheeled artillery and of British cavalry; and rightly arguing that where wheeled artillery could move wheeled transport could follow, insisted on carts being obtained for commissariat purposes. The force selected consisted of one wing of the 3rd Dragoon Guards and four battalions of European infantry. These were the first battalion of the 4th King's Own regiment, the 26th Cameronians, the 33rd, Duke of Wellington's regiment, and the 45th, Sherwood Foresters. These were chosen because they were in quarters near the coast of Bombay, where they could readily be prepared for foreign service, and in case of the prisoners being released, could, without expense, be returned to a peace footing. To these were added four regiments of native Indian cavalry—namely, the 3rd Bombay Light Cavalry, a regiment of the Sind Horse, and the 10th and 12th Bengal Lancers—nine regiments of native Indian infantry, two regiments of Punjab pioneers, and several companies of sappers and miners. The artillery consisted of Major Murray's G battery of the 14th Brigade Royal Artillery, two mountain batteries of Royal Artillery, under the command of Colonel Milward, a Bombay native mountain battery, and a mortar train, with the 5th battery 25th brigade Royal Artillery. A rocket brigade, manned by the sailors of the fleet, was subsequently organised.

The Government of Bombay, as soon as the decision of the Home Government was known, took immediate steps to charter and fit vessels for the transport of troops, animals, and stores. Barges and lighters for landing them on the African coast were prepared, although not in sufficient numbers at first, and in consequence much delay in the landing of stores was incurred. Breech-loading arms and ammunition were demanded from England, and condensing vessels were obtained for the service of the expedition.

But the Commander-in-Chief foresaw that in a barren country, the real stress of the campaign must fall upon the means by which food for the fighting men was to be carried to them. He early directed his attention to the formation of a transport corps, but in its composition was, unfortunately, not allowed to act untrammelled. Sir Robert Napier in August had a plan for the organisation of a transport corps submitted to the Government of Bombay. To this plan the Government objected, on the ground that it threatened to place the Land Transport corps under the control of the Quartermaster-General, while the Government considered that the transport should be controlled by the Commissariat department. Sir Robert Napier cared little under what department the transport corps should be, but claimed for it an efficient military organisation, and proposed that this organisation should be settled by a committee of officers.

From this proposal the Governor of the Presidency dissented, as he said that to two things he felt a great objection—first, that the corps should be organised in a shape that should render it an independent corps instead of being a corps subordinate to the commissariat; secondly, to devolve upon a committee the decision of a point which the Government could very well settle without the intervention of such a body. The Commander-in-Chief, when the Governor objected to the appointment of a committee to prepare a scale of establishment for the land transport, finding that he should be outvoted on every point, and yet be held to have acquiesced in the decision, declined on such terms to share in the councils. Holding aloof from the discussion, he left the Government to appoint some officer or other person to prepare an establishment for the land transport, and merely requested, when any definite form of establishment was resolved upon, that he might have an opportunity of offering an opinion upon it. In October, Sir Robert Napier was allowed an opportunity of inspecting the Land Transport corps, as organised by the Government of Bombay, and immediately wrote to the Governor to say that he felt that in its then disjointed state it would utterly fail to answer its purpose. The lower grades of inspectors were not of character and responsibility sufficient to be capable of managing the mules and mule-drivers, which must often necessarily be detached under their charge, and there was no class provided that could teach them and their subordinates the proper care of their animals and their equipments; nor was there any guarantee that the food of the animals which would be under their care when detached, would be properly applied. Intermediate grades were required between the second inspectors and head muccadums* to connect the chain of responsibility, and the want of a military element also augured a total want of the principle of order and discipline. Sir Robert Napier having already failed to obtain the organisation for his transport which he desired, suggested, however, that instead of the proposed establishment of four head inspectors, eight second inspectors, and sixteen head muccadums for a division of 2,000 mules, the establishment should be four head inspectors, four second inspectors, ten third inspectors, and twenty head muccadums, and that the inspectors should be drawn from the non-commissioned officers of British and native regiments. This, after some delay, was agreed to, but much valuable time had been lost; and as the military element of control was very insufficient, it was found afterwards necessary, under the pressure of disaster, to reorganise the establishment on African soil, while the expedition was delayed by want of transport. While such was the course which was adopted in arranging the controlling

* Overseers.

element of the Land Transport corps, vigorous measures were taken to obtain animals and drivers. The latter, however, were necessarily taken from the seaports of the Mediterranean and the commercial towns of the East. They were the sweepings of the Eastern world; yet it was over such men that the Government of Bombay declined to place any effective supervision. Officers were despatched to the Persian Gulf to purchase mules and hire muleteers. Purchases were made wherever practicable in India, but the principal portion of the mules were obtained on the coast of the Mediterranean. Officers and veterinary surgeons were sent from England to the ports of Spain and the Levant, accredited by the Foreign Office. Aided by the consular agents at those places, they purchased over 8,000 mules. Ten vessels, which were kept cruising for the purpose in the Mediterranean, conveyed these animals to Alexandria, where they were received by Colonel Clarke Kennedy and a detachment of the military train. From Alexandria the mules were sent by railway to Suez, where a depôt was formed. Here they were embarked and conveyed down the Red Sea to Zulla. Pack and draught bullocks were largely collected at Bombay; camels were contracted for at Aden, Hodeida, and neighbouring ports, and elephants were shipped at Bombay for the carriage of artillery. More than 2,000 mules were obtained in the Punjab for transport purposes; whence came, by the sanction of the Government of Bengal, the two military and organised mule trains of Lahore and Rawul Pindee, which afterwards did much useful service. These measures were so vigorously carried out, that between the time when the expedition was decided upon and the fall of Magdála, over 40,000 transport animals were disembarked at Zulla.

The climate of the lowland on the African coast was believed to be more dangerous to European constitutions than that of the most unhealthy stations of India. Hence it was necessary that almost the same large number of followers which, for sanitary reasons, always accompany an Indian army, should be transported to Abyssinia, and should remain with the combatant troops until the latter had at least gained the hills. These caused considerable addition to the amount of tonnage required for the marine transport of the army, but subsequent events showed that this addition had not been made in vain.

CHAPTER III.

RECONNAISSANCE OF THE COUNTRY.

LIEUT.-COL. MEREWETHER, the Political Resident at Aden, foreseeing the inevitable results of Theodore's detention of the captives, had during the early part of 1867 devoted considerable attention to obtaining information concerning Abyssinia. In his exertions in this direction he was aided by Mr. Munzinger, who since 1865 had been the British and French consular agent at Massowah. His experience of the Abyssinian difficulty and constant intercourse with the captives made it only natural to suppose that he would bring valuable information to aid the councils held at Bombay during the preparation of the expedition. Colonel Merewether was ordered to come from Aden. Sir Robert Napier had previously urged the despatch of officers to the African coast to reconnoitre, as well as agents to collect supplies and transport near the point of disembarkation. His proposal was now carried into effect.

The party detached to reconnoitre the coast of Africa and to select a convenient spot for the debarkation of the force, sailed from Bombay on September 16. This party was composed of a committee, attended by an escort of marine infantry and some cavalry. The president of the committee was Lieut.-Colonel Merewether, C.B. The members were Lieut.-Colonel Phayre, Quartermaster-General of the Bombay Army; Lieut.-Colonel Wilkins, Royal Engineers; the senior naval officer, and the senior medical officer. The instructions given to this committee by Sir Robert Napier pointed conclusively to the selection of Annesley Bay as the point to be first examined.* He had foreseen even from Bombay that the routes from Tajurrah and Amphilla Bay would be dangerous to the health of the troops. The lines from these points to the highlands of Abyssinia would have been untenable during the hot weather, and would have led through a country entirely devoid of water and forage. Officers were despatched with the reconnoitring party to draw up special reports, each regarding his own department. The reconnoitring party was authorised to take into employment such portions of the native tribes under Egyptian rule as might be found necessary and expedient for guards for forage parties and escorts.

Colonel Merewether arrived with his committee and escort,† which consisted of one company of the Bom-

* Blue Book, p. 440.

† The whole party consisted of Lieutenant-Colonel Merewether, C.B., Lieutenant-Colonel Phayre, C.B., quartermaster-general, Lieutenant-colonel Wilkins, R.E., Major Mignon, assistant commissary-general, Major Baigrie, assistant quartermaster-general, Captain Goodfellow, R.E.,

bay marine battalion and forty men of the 3rd Cavalry, reached Massowah on October 1, where he remained on the 2nd, and investigated the port and its neighbourhood. It was found that the water near Massowah was totally insufficient for the sustenance of a large force, and that the nearest running water could be reached more quickly and conveniently from Annesley Bay. The reconnoitring party accordingly sailed to that harbour, and landed on October 4 at Mulkutto, a watering place in the delta of the Huddas torrent, near Zulla, the ancient Adulis. Here appeared a convenient landing place, except that the western coast of Annesley Bay trends so gently to the water that boats could not approach the land, and a great part of the shore was covered by water at spring tides. The vicinity of the mountains through which a road had to be found to the highlands, and the presence of some water, decided Colonel Merewether to select Zulla as the landing place for the army. The horses and animals were disembarked with some difficulty, and preparations made to survey the neighbouring country. The first step taken was with the object of finding a passage through the mountains to the tableland; with this view the Huddas and Komayli defiles were re-

Captain Pottinger, R.A., Lieutenant Jopp, R.E., Lieut. Mortemer, R.A., Lieutenant Henriel, Surgeon Lumsdaine, Assistant-surgeon Martin, 1 company Marine battalion, 8 men, sappers and miners, 3 draughtsmen, 5 guides, 35 tent lascars, 136 public followers, 93 private followers, 40 men 3rd Bombay Light Cavalry, 149 mules.

connoitred. In the latter water was found at the foot of the mountains, about fourteen miles from Zulla. Colonel Phayre pushed up the Komayli Pass, and on October 11 found water at Sooro. The pass was extremely difficult, but it was seen that with labour it could be made fit even for the passage of an army. Colonel Phayre perceived this, and urged that the work of making a road through the difficulties of the defile should be undertaken at once. By the middle of October the water at Zulla failed, and all the cavalry and infantry of the reconnoitring party had to be sent to Adoda, to encamp there, where some existed. The instructions of the Commander-in-Chief to the reconnoitring party warned them against any route that would not lead by the shortest line to the highlands, or that would entail a change of the connecting posts in the hot weather; but Colonel Merewether believed that a route might be found from the southern extremity of Annesley Bay to the highlands, which would be shorter than that by Komayli. On October 21 he started to make investigations in this direction, but the route was found so difficult and impracticable that, after wasting nearly fifteen days, it had to be given up. It was unfortunate when time was so valuable that Colonel Phayre's recommendation with regard to the Senafe Pass had not at once been acted upon.

In the meantime, the advanced brigade of the expedition, under the command of Colonel Field, 10th Native Infantry, was despatched from Bombay, arrived in Annesley Bay on October 21, and landed on October 30. It consisted of the 3rd Regiment of Bombay Light Cavalry, No. 1 company of Bombay Native Artillery, with a mountain train, Nos. 3 and 4 companies Bombay Sappers and Miners, the 10th Regiment of Native Infantry, a division of the Land Transport corps, and some of the Commissariat corps. This force was designed by Sir Robert Napier to act as a guard for the establishment of magazines and depôts on the seacoast, and to assist generally in necessary works. About the same time arrived also Captain Edye, R.N., with H.M.S. 'Satellite,' who immediately made valuable arrangements for condensing water to supply the troops and animals on shore. Early in November, Colonel Merewether undertook a thorough survey of the Komayli Pass, and reached a point about nine miles from Senafe; farther he could not penetrate, as it was for political reasons undesirable that as yet he should enter Abyssinian territory, or come into contact with Abyssinian people. The survey of the pass, however, was so favourable that as soon as Colonel Merewether returned to Zulla he ordered up working parties to improve the road in the pass, and to commence a passage through the most difficult obstacles. Not satisfied with the pass which he had discovered to be practicable for the passage of the army, Colonel Merewether spent some time in investigating the Huddas Pass, which leads to Tekonda, but found it much more difficult than that by Komayli. Colonel Merewether then resolved to move the advanced brigade to the highlands, to occupy Senafe and cover the issue of the defile. It was also advisable to move the cavalry away from the plains, as an epidemic had broken out among the horses, from which many died. On December 2 Colonel Merewether picked up the 10th Native Infantry at Sooro, and with that regiment and the Bombay mountain train occupied Senafe on December 5. The 3rd Cavalry came up on the following day.

When it was foreseen that an expedition to Abyssinia was inevitable, a letter was written by Lord Stanley to King Theodore, the purport of which was that remonstrances having failed to obtain the release of the captives, the matter had been placed in the hands of Sir Robert Napier. This letter was sent in quadruplicate to the political resident at Aden, who had orders to forward its different copies by different messengers from Massowah to the court of Theodore.

Sir Robert Napier was also ordered to make a demand for the captives from Theodore as he thought fit. Lord Stanley's letter reached Colonel Merewether at Zulla on October 10, who despatched it to Mr. Rassam, by whom it was ultimately destroyed for fear of the effects it might have upon Theodore's temper. By order of Sir Robert Napier, Colonel Merewether dis-

tributed a message * to the people of Abyssinia and a
proclamation to Theodore in the country, the purport
of which was that the British force came to make war

---

* The following is the text of the message and proclamation :—

*From Lieutenant-General Sir Robert Napier, Commander-in-Chief,
Bombay Army.*

To THEODORUS, KING OF ABYSSINIA,—

I am commanded by Her Majesty the Queen of England to demand
that the prisoners whom your Majesty has wrongfully detained in captivity shall be immediately released and sent in safety to the British
Camp.

Should your Majesty fail to comply with this command, I am further
commanded to enter your Majesty's country at the head of an army to
enforce it, and nothing will arrest my progress until this object shall
have been accomplished.

My Sovereign has no desire to deprive you of any part of your dominions, nor to subvert your authority, although it is obvious that such
would in all probability be the result of hostilities.

Your Majesty might avert this danger by the immediate surrender of
the prisoners.

But should they not be delivered safely into my hands, should they
suffer a continuance of ill-treatment, or should any injury befall them,
your Majesty will be held personally responsible, and no hope of future
condonation need be entertained.

R. NAPIER, Lieut.-General,
Commander-in-Chief, Bombay Army.

To THE GOVERNORS, THE CHIEFS, THE RELIGIOUS ORDERS, AND THE
PEOPLE OF ABYSSINIA.

It is known to you that Theodorus, King of Abyssinia, detains in
captivity the British Consul Cameron, the British Envoy Rassam, and
many others, in violation of the laws of all civilised nations.

All friendly persuasion having failed to obtain their release, my Sovereign has commanded me to lead an army to liberate them.

All who befriend the prisoners or assist in their liberation shall be
well rewarded, but those who may injure them shall be severely punished.

When the time shall arrive for the march of a British army through
your country, bear in mind, People of Abyssinia, that the Queen of England has no unfriendly feelings towards you, and no design against your
country or your liberty.

against Theodore alone, and that no peaceful inhabitant of Abyssinia would be molested.

In consequence of this proclamation, Colonel Merewether had hardly established himself at Senafe when he received friendly communications from Kassai, the lieutenant of Wagshum Gobaze, who had rebelled against his chief, and installed himself as governor of Tigre. Kassai sent to the British camp Murcha Werke, the son of an Armenian who had resided in Abyssinia, who had himself been educated as a missionary by Dr. Wilson, at Bombay, and spoke English exceedingly well. A letter was also received at the same time from the Wagshum himself.

During the first few days of December, the Sind brigade from Kurrachee arrived in Annesley Bay under the command of Brigadier Collings. It consisted of the 33rd British regiment, the Belooch regiment of Bombay infantry, the Sind Horse and Murray's Armstrong battery. At the same time Sir Charles Staveley arrived with orders from Sir Robert Napier to dissolve the committee of which Colonel Merewether was presi-

---

Your Religious establishments, your persons, and property shall be carefully protected.

All supplies required for my soldiers shall be paid for.

No peaceable inhabitant shall be molested.

The sole object for which the British Force has been sent to Abyssinia is the liberation of Her Majesty's subjects.

There is no intention to occupy permanently any portion of the Abyssinian Territory, or to interfere with the government of the country.

R. NAPIER, Lieut.-General,
Commander-in-Chief, Bombay Army.

October 26, 1867.

dent, and to assume supreme command of the forces until the arrival of the Commander-in-Chief himself. Sir Charles Staveley found matters in an unsatisfactory state at Zulla. There was no guiding hand at the port of disembarkation. All the superior officers had remained in the mountains; the result of the faulty organisation of the transport train was evident; from want of discipline and superintendence animals were lost, strayed or stolen, while those that remained were starved from want of food or dying from want of water. The condition of the animals was such that few could accomplish the arduous march to Senafe. Hundreds died on the way, and their bodies quickly mortifying under the blazing sun, threatened to produce direful diseases throughout the whole force. Sir Charles Staveley took instantaneous and vigorous measures: parties of native Shohos were enlisted to burn the carcasses, both at Zulla and in the pass. Some stores were pushed up by vigorous means to Senafe, where the troops, through the failure of the transport corps, were threatened with starvation. The Belooch regiment was sent into the defile to clear a road in the most difficult places. Some sort of order was restored. For nearly a month, until relieved by Sir Robert Napier, Sir Charles Staveley remained in command. During that time two batteries of mountain guns arrived from England, and the gunners to man them from Bombay; the 4th (King's Own) British regiment also arrived, as did the 3rd Bombay Native Infantry, the 25th Bombay Native Light Infantry, a regiment of Punjab pioneers, and two companies of Madras sappers. A pier was commenced, which projected for some nine hundred feet into the sea, but it was built with great difficulty, as there was no stone in the Zulla coast, and all had to be brought from the island of Dissee, some ten miles distant. A tramway was laid down to connect the extremity of the pier with the commissariat camp and the ordnance department. At the end of the pier and on a small artificial island, some three hundred yards farther south, two fixed condensers were placed, which, with the shipping in harbour, were by the beginning of January able to supply one hundred and sixty tons of fresh water daily, of which one hundred and twenty tons were daily placed on shore for the use of men and animals. A second pier, for the sole use of the commissariat department, was also commenced. Two large wooden sheds, for commissariat stores, were commenced, and rations were collected at Zulla for 2,000 Europeans for three months and for 7,000 natives for six months. By means of these vigorous measures to supply food and water, the epidemic which had been raging among the horses and transport animals was much decreased, and the organisation of the Land Transport corps was daily improved.

CHAPTER IV.

SIR R. NAPIER AT ZULLA.

ON the afternoon of January 2, 1868, Her Majesty's ship 'Octavia' steamed slowly into Annesley Bay, picked her way carefully through the fleet of transport vessels which rocked heavily on the monotonous swell, and dropped anchor opposite to the landing place of Zulla. On board of this vessel were Sir Robert Napier and General Malcolm, with several staff officers. Annesley Bay is formed by nature to be a first-rate harbour. Its entrance is on the north. But the waves raised by the northerly winds, which sweep savagely down the Red Sea, are debarred from agitating its waters. They break in harmless foam upon the low bare coral island of Dissee, which lurks as a sentinel at the mouth of the bay. On the east it is separated from the sea by the low promontory of Birri, which stretches out from the foot of the hills to leave only a narrow passage between its farthest point and the island of Dissee. On the eastern shore, the high mountains of Abyssinia press at the southern bend of the bay close down to the water's edge, but trending away in their northward course, leave a flat alluvial plain, fourteen miles wide, between their lowest spurs and the water's edge. This plain is bounded on the north by the sandy chain of Mount Gedam, which runs from the main chain of hills down to the sea opposite the island of Dissee. The plain is formed in the lap of the mountains by the alluvial deposits of the Huddas and Komayli torrents; it is thickly covered with the shrubs of the salt-plant, and on it are found the ruins of the ancient Greek colony of Adulis. The name has been corrupted by the pronunciation of the nomad Danakil tribes who roam the plain into Zulla. Those who gazed from the deck of the 'Octavia' could perceive upon this plain a thick congregation of white canvas tents glistening in the tropical sun. Here and there a few scarlet coats showed the presence of British soldiers, and the ensign of England floated lazily from a tall flagstaff in one portion of the camp. Down by the water's edge a rude wharf was in course of construction, and near it lay crowds of boats and barges eager to discharge their teeming cargoes of merchandise of war. Hundreds of boats sped between the coast and the vessels of the transport fleet. Crowds of workmen on the shore toiled to carry the discharged cargoes from the water's edge to the commissariat depôt. Condensers were at work pumping with their whirring machinery salt water from the sea and urging it out again fit for drinking towards the land. Beyond this busy scene, the low plain, studded with stunted shrubs, spread towards the mountains, which shot from their heavy masses, sprinkled with numerous acacia, their clear-cut edges into the sky.

Sir Robert Napier was not able to land. The fatigue of preparation had told on his usually hardy constitution. For a few days he was sick, but fortunately not for long. Nevertheless, he assumed personal command of the forces, and on the 5th was able to disembark, and to minutely scrutinise the state of preparation at Zulla. On January 7, the Commander-in-Chief landed in state. The yards of the 'Octavia' were manned by long rows of white-clad seamen, who stood rigid and firm against the deep blue sky. As his barge pulled away from the side of the man-of-war, the guns bellowed a parting salute, which was answered back as he neared the shore by the milder reports of a mountain battery. On the wharf a guard of honour was drawn up to receive him, and while the soldiers presented arms, and the officers lowered their swords to greet their chief, the commander of the British expedition to Abyssinia stepped on the African shore.

The low plain on which the British camp was pitched stretches for about fourteen miles from the sea to the foot of the mountains. Through these mountains there are two passes which lead to the Abyssinian highlands. These are formed respectively by the ravines cut through the hills by the Huddas and Komayli torrents. During the rainy season, which lasts from May till September, these torrents are for short times formidable masses of water, which rush down the passes, carrying away rocks, stones, and trees in their headlong course. During the remaining months of the year the passes are nearly dry—available as roads; and even in the rainy season it is probable that small numbers of careful travellers lightly equipped could pass up and down the Komayli Pass with safety, for this torrent drains no large portion of the highlands. Water is found in the passes only at rare intervals, and then in small quantities. The Pass of Komayli, which was shorter than the Huddas route by about ten miles, was selected for the march of the army. The road led along the bed of the torrent. When this route was first investigated by the reconnoitring party, it was barely practicable for the passage of animals. At Komayli the road entered the mountains: this point lies about fourteen miles from Zulla. Here a station was established, as a halting place for troops and transport animals. Deep wells were dug, and by great labour sufficient water was found for the requirements of the passing detachments. At Komayli the road entered the mountains, but for about three miles farther ran nearly level. The defile in this part was about a quarter of a mile broad. The sides of the watercourse, which itself was wide but filled with large water-rolled stones and loose shingly gravel, were covered with prickly acacia trees that ran up the mountain side. Three miles from Komayli the ascent began. The track took to the dry bed of the torrent, and twisted painfully through large boulder rocks and débris washed down from the hills. The mountains drew more towards each other, rising more precipitously and to a greater height till at Lower Sooro, ten miles beyond Komayli, they press so close upon the river bed as to leave only a fissure of a few yards through which the water could force its way. The confined torrent, in its desperate struggles to escape, had washed down rocks, torn deep holes, and piled mighty stones in wild confusion in the narrow pass. Through this chaotic mass the road had to be driven, as the cliffs rose up sheer on either hand, hanging inwards, as if yearning to clasp each other to their craggy bosoms, and to close altogether the narrow fissure which some convulsion of nature had rent through their bowels. So steep and high were their sides that even at mid-day there was a gloom on the tiny rill which, rising at Upper Sooro, trickled down to Lower Sooro, where it was sucked up and lost in the thirsty sand, and the high tropical moon never struck down to its waters, or lit up the contorted scenery through which it wandered. This narrow defile lasted for over two miles, and till the road nearly reached the station of Upper Sooro, where a detachment of the Belooch regiment and some sappers and miners were stationed to make the road through the defile. At the Sooro spring water was found in sufficient quantity to suffice for considerable detachments of men and animals. It was in the Sooro defile that the great difficulty and danger of the road lay; and no pains were spared by the working parties there, under Major Bevill and Lieutenant Sturt, to render it practicable. After six weeks of hard labour, they formed a road perfectly safe for field artillery and wheeled transport; but this road was almost certain to be swept away by the first rains, and while it might be impassable an army on the highlands could obtain no supplies from the shipping at Zulla. It would then have to depend upon what the country could produce, and what might have been stored at Senafe. Although supplies were at first obtained to some extent at Senafe from the country people, in a few days their resources were exhausted. The Commander-in-Chief therefore spared nothing to provision the post which must be the sheet-anchor of his operations.

It was with a sense of relief that a traveller left the iron fastnesses of Sooro to emerge again into a broader though hardly less barren portion of the pass. For thirteen miles the road, ascending steeply, twined along the stony watercourse, until it reached the station of

Undul Wells. Here a well was sunk, from which, by means of chain pumps, one hundred gallons of water could be hourly drawn; but this was not sufficient to water the large convoys which daily passed towards Senafe, and more wells had to be sunk after the first visit of the Commander-in-Chief to the station. Above Undul Wells there was a small plain in the pass which, from the number of birds of that kind found there, received the name of Guinea-Fowl Plain. Here the previous desert character of the pass was lost, and a beautiful vegetation commenced. The tulip tree of enormous size, the acacia, and the oleander clustered along the side of the way. The cactus rose stiff and hard among schistose rocks. Animals were abundant. The antelope occasionally bounded across the road; the boar and elephant had their haunts in the hills beside. Baboons and monkeys barked and gibbered from the cliffs, and crowds of bright humming birds flashed their gorgeous plumage in the dazzling sunlight.

Guinea-Fowl Plain passed, the road quickly ascended, and after eighteen miles of steady climbing reached a difficult defile near Raha Guddy, where a road was pioneered with some difficulty by a wing of the Belooch regiment, under Captain Hogg. The station of Raha Guddy lay more than 6,000 feet above Zulla, and about 4,000 feet above Sooro. Here the nights were cold, and heavy dew fell. Fires were welcome after sunset, and fortunately plenty of firewood was available. From Raha Guddy eight miles of quick ascent led on to the table-land of Senafe. Part of this ascent passed over a very steep and tangled hill-side, known as the Senafe Ghat. There a cooler climate was reached, and the altered vegetation marked the elevation, for cypress junipers grew freely, and their silvery boughs across the dusty path afforded now and again a momentary relief from the hot African sun, which even at this height burnt fiercely in the daytime.

At Senafe, which lay over 7,000 feet above the level of the sea, as soon as the sun went down the heat ceased. Warm clothing and heavy blankets were immediately required, for the nights were very cold. The great variation of temperature of necessity caused an increase in what it was least desirable to increase— baggage. But the troops had to be clothed for two opposite climates, and as their health must be preserved, their warm clothing and heavy blankets had to be carried.

Senafe had been occupied by Colonel Merewether, to whom the local rank of Brigadier-General was given, with the advanced brigade on December 6. Since that time, before the arrival of Sir Robert Napier, considerable exertions had been made to open a practicable road between the head of the pass and the sea-coast, but in many places the rugged bed of the watercourse had been untouched. Sir

Robert Napier found great difficulty in obtaining accurate information of either the state of the road or the condition of the Land Transport corps in the pass, until he despatched one of the officers of his personal staff, who had orders to travel day and night to Senafe and back, making notes of the road and mustering every animal of the transport train, either standing or travelling in the Komayli Pass. The report of this officer was laid before Sir Robert Napier, who immediately issued stringent orders for the rectification of affairs, to which the troops engaged as working parties nobly responded. It was soon marvellous to see what was done; a good road was quickly made as far as Komayli over the sandy plain, and the railway was pushed forward in the same direction; between Komayli and Sooro, the road already practicable for pack animals was widened, and formed with easy gradients, and cleared for the passage of carts. Through the tangled boulders of the Sooro defile the skill of the Bombay sappers and the ready labours of the Beloochees raised a carriage way, which amply sufficed for the passage of artillery, and the Senafe Ghat was made practicable by a fine display of engineering talent. The Komayli Pass daily lost some of its horrors. Till after the arrival of Sir Robert Napier the pack animals, which formed the convoys of the transport train, had to carry their own forage, which diminished materially the load they could bear and decreased proportionately their useful labour. Grass was then by the active agency of the intelligence department of head-quarters found in some off-shooting valleys near Sooro, Undul Wells, and Raha Guddy, which was sufficient to forage the animals as they passed those places, and they were consequently able to carry a larger useful load. In his instructions to the reconnoitring party, Sir Robert Napier had enjoined the use of native carriage, by means of which he had hoped that the Commissariat Department would have been able to accumulate supplies at Senafe before his arrival. But when he reached Zulla, he found that the whole available means of transport were strained to feed the small force then at Senafe. Arrangements were then made to supplement the pack transport with wheeled carriages, and their introduction first allowed the supplies of the commissariat at Senafe to gain ground over the daily consumption of the garrison. It was found that each pack animal could not carry more than 190 lbs., of which 40 lbs. was required for his own grain to feed him on the road. In draught the same animal could draw, even on the steep roads of the pass, 3 cwt., or 336 lbs., besides his grain. A great addition was consequently made to the daily supply of provisions to Senafe by the introduction of wheeled transport. At first Sir Robert Napier retained all the troops near the sea, except those which were already established as a necessary guard to cover the issue of the defile, and to protect the accumulation of commissariat stores at Senafe. The epidemic which attacked horses in the low ground, required that cavalry should be pushed up to the highlands, and the Sind Horse was consequently sent up, but the 4th British regiment, the two mountain batteries under Milward, the 3rd Bombay Native Infantry, the 25th Bombay Native Light Infantry, some of the 23rd Punjab Pioneers, and two companies of Madras Sappers were held on the sea-coast, while the remainder of the troops which were to compose the force were ordered not to sail for Zulla until matters had been made more favourable for their reception. The guns and gunners of Murray's Armstrong batteries were stationed at Komayli, while the horses and drivers were sent to join the advanced force, which, under General Malcolm, consisting of the 33rd Regiment, Marrett's native mountain train, the 10th Native Infantry, and 3rd Bombay Cavalry, held Senafe and the head of the pass. In the defile, working on the road and garrisoning the stations along the line of seventy miles between Zulla and the highlands, were the Beloochees, the 10th company Bengal Engineers, the Bombay marine battalion, the Bombay Sappers, and a detachment of the 23rd Punjab Pioneers. Sir Robert Napier despatched the celebrated African traveller, Major Grant, who was one of the officers of the intelligence department at head-quarters, to Prince Kassai, at Adowa, in return for the embassy of Murcha Werke, and with the object of persuading the Prince of Tigre to let his people open up markets of supplies for the army. The latest intelligence received from the captives before the Commander-in-Chief moved from Zulla was dated December 18, and described Theodore as moving very slowly with heavy ordnance and baggage from Debra Tabor towards Magdâla. Many thought that while Theodore was executing this movement, the army of Sir Robert Napier could have acted upon his flank, or have interposed between him and his fortress. Such a movement theoretically appeared admirable, but practically Senafe was 340 miles from Magdâla. The intelligence which was sent by the captives on December 18 from Magdâla left Theodore's camp on the 3rd of that month, and it expressly stated by the sacrifice of his heavy ordnance, Theodore could reach Magdâla in four or five days. On December 3 not a single British soldier was at Senafe, and the road through the Komayli defile was almost impracticable for the passage of any quantity of stores or provisions. On the 6th only a weak detachment had reached the highlands, and there were no reserves worth speaking of at Zulla; the gunners of the rifle mountain batteries had not arrived, and it would have been impossible to have reached Theodore before he took refuge in Magdâla had all the troops in Abyssinia been ready to start at the date when this intelligence reached Zulla, which was January 3. But they were not ready to move—they had no supplies. Senafe was not provisioned, and to advance without a store there would have been madness. Had the Land Transport corps when landed in Annesley Bay been in complete working order, and had abundant supplies been sent early from Bombay, Senafe might have been provisioned by the beginning of January. But the Land Transport corps was landed in anything but complete working order. What organisation the Transport corps did possess when it left Bombay was lost through the want of proper superintendence, and by its being despatched in driblets to Abyssinia, where consequently, notwithstanding the most heroic exertions of the officers who were attached to it, it was found quite unable to do its work; and at the close of January its deficiencies were being corrected and its organisation assimilated to that which would, had Sir Robert Napier's advice been accepted, have been in complete working order in the beginning of October. Neither had supplies arrived from Bombay in sufficient quantity, nor could those which were actually in harbour be landed sufficiently quickly from the ships on account of the want of lighterage which had been requested early by Sir Robert Napier, but from motives of economy had not been sanctioned at Bombay till a late period of the preparations. Hence there was great delay in commencing operations, which was unavoidable on the spot, but might have been guarded against beforehand. Some not present urged that the force which the Commander-in-Chief judged to be necessary and for which he waited was too large. These chided at the magnitude of the army, but forgot that a line of communication of 400 miles in length had to be held open between Magdála and Zulla, and a chain of fortified posts established to cover the stores and depôts along it. They omitted from consideration that although the natives appeared friendly as long as the expedition was successful and had power, the slightest reverse would convert them all into enemies: that among the Danakil tribes of the mountains the taking of human life is the sole proof of manhood and the sole passport to marriage; and that the uncertain Kassai, Prince of Tigre, hung upon the right flank with 10,000 men at Adowa. He feared to befriend the British, as they had openly proclaimed that, the prisoners secured, they would quit the country, and that their allies would then receive no aid from them against the vengeance of Theodore; and not improbably he wished to delay the advance of the expedition in the hopes that Theodore might in the meantime destroy his rival the Wagshum Gobaze. The other provincial chiefs had also, not unnaturally, a dislike to commit themselves too deeply with an ally whose success would be the signal for their desertion. If any reverse had befallen the

British arms, it is more than probable that all those who had at any time dallied with proposals of alliance would have united against the foreign enemy, and have sought, by an attack on their flank or rear, to strike them a heavy blow, and so avert the coming wrath of Theodore from themselves. It was necessary that the expedition should have its line of communication well guarded and firmly secured. The only means of having it so was by strong posts, which entailed garrisons, which entailed troops.

While the Commander-in-Chief halted at Zulla, vigorous measures were taken to introduce new beneficial arrangements, and to perfect those already existing. The water supply was the first consideration, and by the establishment of a judicious supervision, it was rendered sufficient for not only the animals and troops already at Mulkutto, but also for all those expected. An officer was sent to Egypt to purchase remount horses for the cavalry to replace the horses which had died from the epidemic. Orders were sent to Egypt to continue the purchase of transport animals; requests were sent to Bombay to send out Indian muleteers. By the end of January, the railway was pushed on half way to Komayli, the telegraph was completed to Sooro, shipping was despatched to bring camels from the coast of Arabia, extensive purchases of animals were made in the country. The disembarkation of these was carried on energetically by means of seven large barges, four tugs, three steam launches, and one hundred and sixty native boats; but the second pier for the commissariat department, owing to the want of skilled labour, progressed slowly. During the early part of January the disciplined and organised mules of Lahore and Rawul Pindee arrived from Kurrachee, and were of great assistance. By their aid and the vigorous measures taken by the Commander-in-Chief, it was possible on January 18 to push forward a detachment and occupy Goonagoona, some twelve miles beyond Senafe. Then preparations began to be made for a general advance; exertions were redoubled to get provisions to the highlands. The transport, and consequently baggage, of every officer and man was reduced to the smallest possible dimensions. Officers vied with each other in discarding any article which could be spared, for all thirsted to facilitate the advance of the army. Things which in many campaigns would have been regarded as necessary, were ungrudgingly thrown aside, and in the common cause every personal sacrifice was cheerfully made. By January 25, the Commander-in-Chief considered matters sufficiently forwarded to justify the commencement of an advance on Antalo. Requests were accordingly sent to Aden to push forward the troop-ships which might be coming up from India. The troops which were to compose the force, and which had not arrived, consisted of the 3rd

Dragoon Guards and the two regiments of native lancers from Bengal, the 10th and 12th, the 21st Punjab Pioneers from Bengal, the infantry of the third brigade under Brigadier Schneider, consisting of the 45th Regiment, the 2nd Regiment Bombay Native Infantry, and the 8th Regiment Bombay Native Infantry, as well as the fourth brigade under Brigadier D. M. Stewart, which consisted of the 26th Cameronians, the 5th Regiment Bombay Native Light Infantry, and the 18th Regiment Bombay Native Infantry.

On January 25, a brigade under Brigadier Collings, which consisted of a wing of the 33rd Regiment, a wing of the 10th Native Infantry, a detachment of sappers and miners, and a wing of the Sind Horse, was ordered to hold itself in readiness to march from Senafe on Antalo. On the 25th, the Commander-in-Chief left Zulla for the front, and orders were given for the troops still at Zulla to be prepared to march. Sir Charles Staveley remained on the coast, for at Zulla beat the heart from which the life-stream flowed that must pulsate through the long artery of the line of communications, and carry food to the farthest outposts; but General Russell was ordered up from Aden to relieve Staveley, who was required in the front, and to assume the control of the landing-place. And this was no light task, for the army throughout the campaign depended almost entirely for everything, except meat and firewood, on the ships and on the Senafe depôt stored from the harbour. Never were operations carried on in a country so unfavourable to war: the very base of operations, where at the end of January there was a population of about 12,000 men and animals, had to be supplied with water from the condensers and from the shipping. An accident to a delicate piece of machinery, or the breaking of the valve of a pump, caused the stock of the precious fluid to run short, and inflicted a great inconvenience in the camp, where the water had to be doled out in daily portions of limited quantity, and a reduction of the ration told heavily on man and beast. A storm of sufficient severity to drive the condensing ships from their anchorage would have caused a terrible calamity. To provide against such an accident, every effort was made to provide a reserve of water in a great reservoir, which was formed partly of ships' tanks and partly of a tank sent in pieces from England and put together on the spot. There was no timber in the country, there was no stone near the sea-coast; every block of coral and every beam of wood for the construction of piers or storehouses had to be imported; every inch of rope had to be brought from the ships; every yard of road had to be made to allow the convoys to pass; every boat had to be brought to the coast for the disembarkation of troops and stores, for none were found there, though a liberal supply was expected by some who should have been better informants. The boats that there were could not at first approach the beach, as the water shoaled slowly and the beach was very flat. Not the least arduous of the duties of the campaign was the disembarkation of the cargoes of the ships; and its success was much due to the exertions of Captain Tryon, R.N., who with limited means achieved great things. Throughout the expedition there was the most complete cordiality between the army and navy. In some former expeditions this had not been the case. Here, however, Commodore Heath, his officers and men, threw themselves heart and soul into the work of forwarding the progress of the army—did right good work, and did it nobly. It was satisfactory to the navy as well as to the army, that a Naval Brigade was organised while the Commander-in-Chief halted at Zulla, which was placed under the command of Captain Fellowes, R.N., of Her Majesty's ship Dryad. The men of the Naval Brigade were armed with cutlasses and Snider carbines, and their mules carried rocket tubes, which were of great aid in the capture of Magdála.

Before the date when the Commander-in-Chief left Zulla, a large detachment of the Army Works corps and of the Bengal Cooley corps arrived. The former were immediately set to work to push forward the railway: the latter arrived with fever on board their vessel, and had to be sent to a separate sanitary camp for some time, but were afterwards of great service. When Sir Robert Napier left for Senafe, the state of matters was much improved. He had carried out strenuously the reforms commenced by Sir Charles Staveley. The condition of the Land Transport had been accurately ascertained and much ameliorated. The difficulty of provisioning Senafe was being gradually overcome; the road was being made rapidly available for wheeled carriages, and convoys of carts were already plying to Komayli. The supply of water at the station of Undul or Maiyen wells had been doubled, and still more wells were being sunk. Grass had been found near Senafe, and large stores of it collected in that place, as the troops cut it and the cavalry horses brought it up. Every man that could labour, and every beast that could walk, did his daily labour for his daily bread. The Commander-in-Chief set the example: he remained toiling on the hot sea-coast, and did not, until his troops were ready to advance, seek the more delightful and pleasant climate of the highlands. He took almost no rest, but he infused a similar spirit in every man in his army—all followed in the same course, and every soldier worked as few labourers work at home. Those whose great theory it has been to hold that the British soldier is helpless, should have paid a visit to the sea-coast of Annesley Bay. And what work it was! Under a burning sun, and in a tropical climate, with an apportioned allowance of water, with perpetual clouds of dust lodging in every pore, physical labour was excessively severe. But the railway and roads had to be made, and made they were.

The railway did not make such rapid progress as was expected. Locomotives had, however, been landed, and were useful in the removal of commissariat stores from the piers to the storehouses.

CHAPTER V.

ADVANCE TO ADIGERAT.

ON the 25th January Sir Robert Napier left the sea-coast, and, after minutely inspecting all the stations in the pass, arrived at Senafe on the 29th. By the time the Commander-in-Chief left Zulla friendly relations had been opened with Kassai, the ruler of Tigre, and Major Grant had been sent to Adowa to make arrangements with that Prince for the supply of provisions to the army during its passage through his dominions. An agreement had also been made with fourteen chieftains of tribes inhabiting the pass through the mountains not only to allow of the free passage of convoys through their fastnesses, but to carry on native cattle some of the supplies required by the troops from the plains to the table-land. The Naval Brigade had been landed and encamped on shore, and naval officers had been appointed to act as pilots for vessels through the intricate channels which lead to Annesley Bay. The Egyptian governor of Massowah, who had been anything but conciliatory towards the political officers of the expedition, had been removed by the Egyptian Admiral who visited Annesley Bay. His degradation was merited;

for, in violation of the opinions expressed by his Government, he had told the natives not to help the British, but to plunder them, and was not without cause believed to be intriguing to induce Kassai to oppose the expedition. The railway gear had arrived from Bombay, but was inconveniently packed in the vessels which conveyed it, and required much time to deliver. The engines were for the most part old and bad; the rails were of different patterns and difficult to lay from want of platelayers, who had to be improvised from the troops, in aid of the few sent from Bombay. Messages were sent to the chiefs of the Daunt and Dalanta tribes to cut Theodore off from Magdala; but a few days after the despatch of the messengers, news arrived of the submission of these chiefs to Theodore, which left him a free passage to his fortress. On the 25th January a brigade consisting of the 33rd Regiment, a wing of the 10th Native Infantry, a mountain battery, a wing of the Sind Horse and a detachment of Sappers, was placed under orders to advance towards Antalo, and on the 30th of that month the British vanguard occupied Adigerat, thirty-six miles beyond Senafe. Goonagoona, Mai Magrab, and Focada, three stations on the road between Senafe and Adigerat, were also occupied by infantry, cavalry, and engineers, who were engaged in making the road practicable for laden transport animals and guns. In the few days after the arrival of the Commander-in-Chief, the 4th King's Own Regiment and the steel mountain batteries arrived at Senafe, and other troops moved up in succession to replace those sent farther into the country. The road from the coast was, by the exertions of the Bombay Sappers and Miners, the Belooch battalion, and the 23rd Punjab Pioneers, made practicable for wheels throughout its entire length, and on the last day of January a convoy of seventy-five bullock carts arrived safely with commissariat stores at the highland post. The importance of this change in the method of transport was great, as two animals in draught could drag 750 lbs. from Zulla to Senafe, while two pack animals could only carry 380 lbs., of which not a little was required for their own forage.

Senafe may be regarded as the secondary base of operations in the campaign. It was the great storehouse for supplies and provisions, which, after being carried through the Komayli pass, were to be pushed on to the front. The camp was situated on the plateau of the Abyssinian highlands, about two miles in front of the issue of the Komayli defile, on some rather elevated rocky ground. On its east rise some high sandstone cliffs scarped and water-worn by the waves of some primeval ocean. On the west the spurs of Mount Sowayra protected the left flank of the camp. In its front extended a wide plain, over which stretched into the distance the military road to Antalo. Beyond the western sandstone cliffs a steep descent of some thousand feet led into the valley of the Marab, over which, to the southward, could be seen the mountains of Adowa. The view across this hollow was magnificent: the country was rugged and broken by jagged masses of schistose rock which raised their jagged edges topped with acacia and juniper trees above the scanty vegetation of the intervening ravines. In the glare of midday this prospect looked hot and thirsty, but in the first glimmerings of early dawn, or when the quickly-setting tropic sun swept down behind the distant hills, it was magnificently grand.

Preparations were made for the security of Senafe, by which the command of the Komayli Pass and the safety of the stores collected there could be insured in case any of the native chiefs might attempt to take advantage of the absence of the main body of the force in the south, and trouble the weakest point of all armies, the line of communications. These precautions were necessary, as there was no doubt that as the expedition showed strength, in the same proportion it gained the friendship of the rulers of the provinces of Abyssinia. For this reason alone, even if for no other, the posts along the line of communications had to be strong. But there were much more powerful reasons: the food of the army depended upon secure and uninterrupted communications, and this security had to be powerfully insured and not left exposed to the stroke of fortune, nor dependent on the caprice of any semi-savage chieftain.

As the army advanced the promised land, where abundant supplies were to be found, receded before it as the mirage in the desert does before the footsteps of the approaching traveller. Senafe was at one time to be the end of all the labours of the transport train, and from its native resources to feed the army. Adigerat was next pointed to, but it also was occupied, and still no supplies worth speaking of, except firewood and meat, could be obtained in the country. Even then it was still asserted by those who painted the prospect in roseate hue that at Antalo would be found a land flowing with grain and abundant water; but by the time that Adigerat was occupied the sceptics in Abyssinian supply were in the majority, and few were sanguine enough to believe that the army would ever be enabled to shake off the weighty chain of communications and move unembarrassed through Southern Abyssinia. Grass was obtained and was bought to a considerable extent. Barley also was purchased, but not in sufficient quantity to supply either the troops or the transport animals. Meat could be obtained, and the wood to cook it was found scattered over the mountain sides; but meat alone in that climate would not suffice for the food of man. Its use as a sole article of food quickly brought on dysentery and scurvy. Vegetables, tea, sugar, and spirits had to be ever in rear of the army, and had to be carried on every day's march. The supplies of these articles required by an army of even small dimensions quickly swells up to an enormous amount and demands a large quantity of carriage. In this latter requisite the force was still unfortunately deficient. Sufficient time had not elapsed to repair an originally defective organisation and the ravages of epidemic among the animals.

The Commander-in-Chief left Senafe on February 3, and marched to Goona-goona. On his road he was met by many chiefs and heads of villages, who tendered to him their friendship and offerings of mead and bread in token of amity. On the 4th he reached Focada, and on the 5th Adigerat. The road from Senafe to Goona-goona ran for some eight miles over the plain in front of the Senafe camp, then bending to the west dived into a valley with steep and lofty sides of sandstone, in which, about four miles on, the watering-place and camp of Goona-goona were situated. Here, for the first time, growing crops were met with. A few patches of green barley not yet ready for the sickle were greeted with delight both as a relief to the monotony of the parched and rocky landscape, and also as an augury of some active cultivation in the country. On the northern side of the valley, perched on an almost inaccessible ledge of rock, was situated the church of Goona-goona, in which some curious paintings and illustrated copies of the Scriptures were met with. From Goona-goona the road rose by a tolerably steep ascent to a breezy upland covered with long dry grass and juniper bushes where the jagged rocks or flat tables of shale did not render all vegetation impossible. Here too were found noble specimens of the red flowering cactus, some growing in thick dwarfed bushes close to the ground, and others rising high like enormous candelabra of red and green foliage. Turning off the table-land, the road was carried along the side of a mountain. This fell precipitously some thousand feet below the narrow path into a deep ravine where, from their distance down, the acacia trees seemed to be tiny shrubs. Above the road the mountain-side was almost equally steep. It was a path where an army might easily have been stopped by a few determined men. For about a mile the road clung to the side of the mountain, and then abutted upon a wide grassy plain, where water was again found near the village of Focada, and the camp and halting-place so named were situated.

The general character of the country and of the people was much the same along the whole length of the route between Senafe and Focada. The former was distinguished by its want of fertility and rugged nature. The villages, of which there were many, were groups of hovels huddled together, sometimes on peaks, sometimes on the talus of high rocks, always upon raised ground; for an Abyssinian's house is his castle, and he has often a difficult task to defend his goods and cattle in a land where the good old border rule still prevails in all integrity. The cottages themselves were built with low walls of mud and stone about eight feet high, and flat roofs of the primitive concrete known as wattle and dab. The inhabitants were tall and of graceful figure, who were met with in crowds on the road carrying barley or honey to market. The troops were kindly in demeanour towards the inhabitants; the discipline of the army was strict; no plundering took place; and no swarthy damsel was subjected to any rude gallantry on the part of the red coats. The Abyssinian men were generally dressed in one single robe of cotton, which appeared seldom to be subjected to the operation of washing. The head men of villages and chiefs of tribes had occasionally a shirt. They wore no head-dress, unless their plaited black hair anointed with rancid butter could be ranked under that designation. They were all armed. The sword, a crooked sickle-like article, worn on the right side, the spear, round shield, and club were their usual weapons; but many had matchlocks, and several possessed double-barrelled guns, by no means despicable, the produce of Birmingham and Liège. The inhabitants of the village of Senafe were Mahommedans, and are said to have been converted to that creed by Arabi Teleki, who visited the village some four centuries ago. The inhabitants of the other villages of Tigre were Christians, and as a mark of their faith wore a blue cord round the throat to distinguish them from followers of the Prophet.

The distance between Focada and Adigerat was about twelve miles. The road led through a country which, compared to that hitherto traversed, might almost be considered fertile. Long grass, dried by constant heat so as to be little but standing hay, waved abundantly along the roadside. Trees were plentiful. Sometimes large cypresses stood alone, at other places the track twined through thick groves of corinda and acacia, while euphorbias were scattered thickly over the sides of the mountains which rose continuously above the way. About six miles from Focada the track, which was throughout easy for a mounted man, rose with a long and gentle slope to the top of a hill, down which, on the other side, it fell abruptly with a steep descent into the valley in which Adigerat is situated. This town was an important strategical point, for here the roads to Adowa and Antalo unite. The town itself was of a better description than any of the villages hitherto seen in Abyssinia. The cottages were built more of stone and less of mud. A church, still in good repair, with a gable instead of the usual flat roof, showed the bounty as well as the religious feeling of one of the late chiefs of Adigerat. His palace stood not far off, but it was in ruins, for intestine wars had within the last few years withered the place, and its rightful ruler lay in prison a captive of Wagshum Gobaze, Prince of Lasta. His wife occupied a small tower surrounded by a mud wall within a few hundred yards of the ruined hall of her husband, where she was said to pine away her life in incessant grief and pinching poverty. Above the town to the west rose the bold mass of Mount Aloquor, and over a 'dip' in this ran the road to Adowa, the capital of Tigre, which lay fifty miles distant.

Major Grant, who had been sent by Sir Robert Napier as an envoy to Kassai, Prince of Tigre, returned on February 7 from Adowa, and joined the Commander-in-Chief at Adigerat. He had been received in a most flattering manner by Kassai; the latter professed, however, to be unable to accompany Major Grant to Adigerat, to pay his respects to the British Commander, as his soldiers were scattered through the villages around his capital, and he feared to leave them lest they should plunder the villagers. He sent presents by one of his councillors, who was received in solemn durbar, and was presented in return with testimonials of friendship in the shape of rugs, knives, and snuff-boxes by the British Commander. The Pioneer Force of the army, consisting of some 200 cavalry, two companies of infantry, and two companies of pioneers, occupied Dolo, about seventy miles south of Adigerat, and within two marches of Antalo, on February 10. Antalo itself was occupied on the 15th by Colonel Phayre with 150 horsemen. The communication between the advanced troops and Adigerat was maintained by small detachments of cavalry, who were posted at convenient spots along the road. On February 11 a column, under Brigadier Collings and Colonel Milward, R.A., was pushed forward from Adigerat to support the Pioneer Force. This column consisted of a wing of the 33rd Regiment, Penn's steel mountain battery, and about 100 sabres of the Sind Horse.

At Adigerat the Commander-in-Chief halted till February 18. He had much to do in that time. There was still a great deficiency of transport, without which the troops could not be supplied, and without supplies they could not move. The country was found to improve slightly in fertility and cultivation as the army pushed forward, but the people were so poverty-stricken by constant civil war that no supplies to support an army, except cattle and sheep, could be obtained from the natives. So attenuated were the resources at this time, that the Deputy-Commissary-General proposed to put the troops on half-rations; but Sir Robert Napier considered that the men, unless sufficiently fed, could not perform the labour expected from them, and declined to entertain the proposal. He was justified in doing so, as the transport train, though still deficient in animals, was daily improving. Several shiploads of camels had been brought from Berbera, but many more pack animals were still required. At this time the troops on the highlands consumed 170 muleloads of provisions daily. It is extremely difficult for those who cannot see it, to realise the immense amount of carriage and the size of convoys required to feed an army in a country where no supplies can be obtained ; and, besides food, there were medicines, hospital establishments, tents, and clothing to be carried, and last, though not least, grain for the sustenance of the horses of the cavalry and artillery and the transport animals themselves, as well as the food of their drivers. And much more remained behind. Depôts and storehouses had to be stocked, not only to replenish the exhausted supplies of the advancing force, but to secure a safe return and to feed the army on its homeward route. At Adigerat an alteration was made in the general organisation of the transport corps. It was separated into two divisions—a highland and lowland. The latter, under the direction of Major Warden, carried supplies from Zulla to Adigerat; the former, under the superintendence of Captain Hand, followed the army, and transported supplies from Adigerat to the combatant troops. The highland train soon became very efficient : it consisted of four divisions of 2,000 mules each, which were subdivided into troops of 150 mules. Its organisation was entirely military, and it worked under the direction of the department of the Quartermaster-General. The two Punjab mule trains were the nucleus of the highland train ; the muleteers were armed and under strict discipline, the superintendents were also armed, and, consequently, the highland train was independent of the regular army for escorts or convoys, or for guards for men cutting grass in a hostile or doubtful country. This train transported all the baggage, ammunition, and supplies between Adigerat and Magdála, as well as on the return march, and proved by its efficiency the advantage and necessity of a military organisation in any army transport corps.

To other matters the Commander-in-Chief had also to turn his attention. Precautions had to be taken for hutting the troops during the rains, which were expected in May, both at Zulla and at the several stations on the Senafe Pass, and on the highlands. Places of refuge had to be provided at frequent intervals in the pass for convoys or detachments, which might be exposed to torrents tearing down the pass in the rainy season. The proper repair of the road had to be insured, and the field telegraph had to be pushed on. The telegraph line by the middle of February was completed to Senafe, but its construction was much impaired by want of poles, for the trees grew so low and so twisted that it was no easy task to find and to cut poles of sufficient length and strength. At Adigerat Sir Robert Napier collected a large supply of poles by the proffer of a dollar for half-a-dozen to the natives; and they were so eager to secure the prized coin that many pulled the timbers out of their houses and brought them into camp, where an officer of the Intelligence Department accepted those suitable, but rejected those which were too small or too light to answer the required purpose. A party of engineer officers was at the same time employed in making an accurate trigonometrical survey while following the march of the army. Every exertion was made to reduce the baggage of the troops to the lightest possible figure. The climate, however, prevented such a reduction as could have been made in an European campaign. On the highlands of Abyssinia the thermometer frequently stood at freezing point at night, and sometimes lower. Warm clothing was absolutely necessary for the troops and followers, and blankets for covering at night could not be dispensed with. The hosts of native followers which accompanied the troops from India had been much diminished before the advance from Zulla, and were further reduced at every subsequent post, as the climate proved them to be much more an encumbrance than a necessity.

While the Commander-in-Chief halted at Adigerat, the 4th Regiment, the Belooch battalion, the 10th Company of Royal Engineers, and Murray's Armstrong battery of Royal Artillery, joined him. At the same time two elephants were brought up to be shown to Kassai at a meeting which it was believed that Prince intended to have with Sir Robert Napier, on the road between Adigerat and Antalo. In Abyssinia the elephants are considered very wild and untameable by the natives, who positively refused to believe that it was possible to reduce them to a state of subordination to man. The passage of the elephants through the country was followed by crowds of wondering and awestruck Abyssinians, who formerly thought that anyone who told them that an elephant could be tamed was dealing in the most flowery romance.

A sensation, second only to that caused by the elephants, was created by the arrival of Murray's battery of Armstrong guns. It was almost doubtful whether it would be possible to get guns over the very difficult road between Senafe and Adigerat. The gunners, however, achieved their task, though not without incurring considerable difficulties.

The latest news received from the captives confined at Magdāla, by the middle of February, was dated the 17th January. At that time Theodore was reported to be within one day's journey of his fortress, but was not expected to arrive at the place, unless he abandoned his baggage and ordnance, before the end of February. He had sent all his prisoners into the fortress.

CHAPTER VI.

ADVANCE TO ANTALO.

AFTER the departure of the column under Brigadier Collings from Adigerat, a battalion of Beloochees, and a company of Sappers and Miners, were pushed forward to repair the road, which Brigadier Collings reported as very bad. Sir Robert Napier himself marched from Adigerat on February 18, with a wing of the 1st battalion of the 4th Regiment, a wing of the 10th Native Infantry, four guns of Murray's Armstrong battery of Royal Artillery, the 3rd Bombay Cavalry, and a detachment of Royal Engineers, and with provisions for thirty days for this force. In two marches he reached Adabagi, where it had been expected that Kassai, Prince of Tigre, would come to have an interview with the British Commander. The Prince did not, however, immediately make his appearance, and a halt was made at Adabagi, partly to give him every opportunity of arriving, but more to allow troops and supplies provided with deficient transport to labour up towards the front. The troops which had advanced beyond Adigerat at this time were the column under Sir Robert Napier, which, with the

Beloochees and Sappers employed on the road, mustered about one thousand men, the Pioneer Force and column under Brigadier Collings, which were together about equally strong, and were collected in the vicinity of Antalo, and a few detached posts of cavalry scattered along the road, which hardly amounted to 100 sabres. At Adigerat itself, which was being converted into a fortified post, there were left in garrison a wing of Native infantry, two of Murray's guns, under Captain Lluellyn, R.A., and two companies of Sappers, who were employed in making the road decently practicable for wheeled carriages down a very difficult and precipitous descent, about four miles north of Adigerat. These were all the troops in front of Senafe, the key of the Komayli Pass, and the great depôt on the highlands. They were not many. Indeed, they did not muster as many sabres and bayonets as an ordinary brigade of a continental army. Yet so weak was the transport, which was only still recovering from the casualties and confusion caused by its originally defective organisation, that no more troops could be sent up to support the advance, for the simple reason that food could not be got forward to supply them with the necessaries of life.

The climate was found so healthy, that at Adabagi the Commander-in-Chief issued orders for the return of nearly all the Indian followers to Zulla, whence those that could not be usefully employed were shipped off to Bombay. This step caused a wonderful improvement in the efficiency and mobility of the army. It relieved the Commissariat Department of the feeding of many thousand mouths, the Transport Train of the carriage of their provisions, and reduced immensely the long lines of baggage and camp followers, which had hitherto toiled for many a mile in rear of the marching columns. A few followers only were retained. These were employed in the hospitals, or were destined for the carriage of sick or wounded : if they had been sent away, fighting men would have had, perforce, to supply their places. Officers' servants were all sent back to Annesley Bay, and the officers were obliged to rely upon such assistance as they might obtain from the soldiery. The troopers of the cavalry were deprived of their syces and grass-cutters, as in the cool climate of the highlands such luxuries were not at all requisite, and their dismissal was of immense aid towards the rapid prosecution of the campaign. An order was also issued by the Commander-in-Chief at Adabagi to reduce the baggage of the force. The troops in front of Adigerat were ordered to deposit all superfluous baggage at Antalo, while those which were to be pushed forward from Senafe left their excess in store at Adigerat. Beyond these two places each officer was restricted to a weight of 75lb. in baggage, in which had to be included his bedding, and the whole of both the necessaries and luxuries of life which he might wish to carry with him. Each soldier was allowed 25lbs., inclusive of bedding. This reduction rendered many animals, previously employed in the carriage of regimental and private baggage, available for the transport of the army's great necessity, food. Its importance may be seen from the following simple statement, that while according to Indian regulations an European battalion would have 1,200 mules for the carriage of its baggage and 600 camp followers, inclusive of muleteers, under the regulations framed by Sir Robert Napier the same battalion could march efficient with 187 mules and under 100 followers. This was an enormous saving in such a country as Abyssinia, where no supplies could be obtained worth speaking of, except meat, which the native Indians hardly eat, and where any day, through the caprice of a petty chieftain, baggage and convoys might have to be carefully guarded. The feeding of the Native followers had hitherto been a great burden on the Commissariat and Transport, for while the European's rations principally consisted of meat, which walked on its own legs, that of the native Indian, consisting of flour, rice, and butter, had to be wholly carried on pack animals.

The road from Senafe to Adigerat was as yet practicable only with the greatest difficulty for wheeled carriages. Murray's guns were, in fact, the only carriages which had, as yet, come over it. The great difficulty lay in the steep descent north of Adigerat. A few carts which attempted the passage here rolled over the hillside, but by the labours of the Sappers under Captain Goodfellow, a good road was constructed here within a few days after the Commander-in-Chief had passed. The road from Adigerat to the south ran for the first five miles up a gently rising valley, bounded on the east by stony hills covered with cactus and acacia, on the west by the towering and precipitous cliffs of Mount Aloquor. Then one of the spurs of the western mountain stretched straight across the valley and barred the way. The labours of the Beloochees made a road up the side of this spur, which was surmounted by a wide plateau of sandstone. After keeping two miles across this plateau, the road suddenly plunged down into a deep and rugged ravine: both down and up the banks of this chasm the way was extremely difficult, and its difficulties had unfortunately been overlooked by the Pioneer Force, which, as a rule, had been more careful in marking out the easy parts of the level that required little labour than in buckling to on the rugged defiles or the steep and broken hills. Here the guns had to be unlimbered to allow them to be got round the sharp angles of the track; horses had to be taken out and led up singly, while the gunners and some of the 10th Native Infantry dragged the guns up by hand for a distance of about half a mile. Beyond this deep ravine the road again passed over a wide plateau, bounded by distant cliffs, which raised their sharp and serrated summits clear against the sky. The plateau itself, clothed with short grass, in which lay enormous numbers of loose stones, and occasionally broken by massive lumps of sheet-rock, bore a slight resemblance to the moorland of the Scottish border. It dipped gently to the camping ground of Mai Wahiz, where a halting-place and watering-station were established. In the neighbourhood of Mai Wahiz there was an appearance of considerable cultivation. In many fields, carefully irrigated by artificial channels from the nearest watercourses, young crops of barley were showing their green shoots above the black loamy soil. It said much for the discipline of the army that when forage was desperately scarce, no horse wandered from the road to feast upon the tempting provender which lay so close within reach. But nowhere was the least damage done to the property of the inhabitants, who extorted enormous prices from the soldiers, and, in return, despised an army which paid and did not take. Honesty was, however, the English General's best policy; for a single day of plunder would have driven the people, with their cattle, into the hills, the supply of meat would have been cut off, and the few provisions which were obtained from the natives could no longer have been procured. Beyond Mai Wahiz the country still improved. About four miles beyond that place the road dropped down a steep descent, where the wheel horses could alone be kept to the guns, and where strong working parties had to be kept to the drag ropes behind to prevent them from rushing down the slope by their mere weight. Then a wide and undulating valley stretched away for about eight miles, covered with high-standing grass, dried and yellowed by the tropic sun. On the left, on some high sandstone cliffs, were perched several ambas, or Abyssinian fortresses, more formidable from their natural position than from their artificial defences. They consisted only of a wall built of stones and mud, at the summit of the precipitous cliff, which is always selected as their site. About nine miles across the plain some low hills were reached, rocky and bare, except for several groves of euphorbias, which sprang up in groups from the few hollows where soil lay thick. In one of these was the camp of Adabagi, where the Commander-in-Chief arrived on February 19, and halted for several days.

During the stay at Adabagi, letters were received from the prisoners at Magdāla, dated January 20, and from Mr. Flad, in Theodore's camp, dated the 19th of the same month. These told that Theodore was still engaged in attempts to get his ordnance and heavy baggage into Magdāla, and that on account of the difficulties of his task, he could not be in the fortress until the first week in March. At this time many chimerical schemes were proposed for rapid advances of the troops, by means of forced marches or of flying columns. The proposers of these ideas forgot, however, that without food troops can neither march nor fight, and as little could be obtained in the country, the army had to depend all but entirely on its transport train and shipping. The former was not yet in such a state as to allow of the rapid advance beyond Antalo of even a diminutive force. Even if it had been, the advance of such a force would have been useless, for it would not have been large enough to protect the convoy, which carried its own provisions, or to efficiently guard one battery of mountain artillery. If it could have repulsed Theodore, it would have been too small to invest Magdála, too weak to attack the place, and would have had to halt in a country entirely devastated by the army of Theodore. If it did not drive Theodore into his fortress, its fighting men might have held their own against him, but he could have cut off its baggage animals, and intercepted its communications with the main body. Such plans emerged from the heated brains of sanguine dreamers, and were not due to a careful calculation of the necessities of war.

On February 23 Sir Robert Napier ordered the small column of about 850 men, which he had brought with him from Adigerat, to be ready to march the following day from its camp at Adabagi towards Antalo. All was prepared for the advance to the south, when, early next morning, intelligence was brought in that Kassai, Prince of Tigre, was advancing towards Hauzzein to seek an interview with the British Commander-in-Chief. Hauzzein lay in the Haramat plain, about twelve miles to the north-west of Adabagi, which itself is about thirty miles south of Adigerat. The order for the advance was at once countermanded, and the force held in readiness to move to meet Kassai. It was arranged that the meeting should take place on the banks of the Diab, a small stream which runs from south to north, about midway between Adabagi and Hauzzein. Soon after daybreak on the 25th, the British troops were under arms, and leaving a hospital guard at Adabagi, moved towards the Diab. The ground was rough and stony, but in the cool morning the troops, accompanied by Murray's guns, quickly traversed the distance, and while the sun was still low, their camp was pitched in some gently undulating ground laden with tall grass, about half a mile from the eastern bank of the Diab. On the further side of the rivulet, which runs between steep and marshy banks, the ground rose for about half a mile in a gentle slope. Here the Abyssinian camp was to be placed, for it was agreed that the rivulet should separate the troops of the two armies. Above this slope some jagged sandstone cliffs beyond Hauzzein rose sharply to the sky, and formed a background to the picture, which was bounded on the right hand and the left by tall, though distant mountains. The sun shone out brightly, and the weather was more than pleasantly warm. Vedettes and signallers were posted towards Hauzzein, to announce the approach of the Tigrean chief, but for some time no report came in to say that he was drawing near.

A little before eleven o'clock, a message came in to tell that the Abyssinian vanguard was in sight. The vedettes and signallers were withdrawn to their own side of the Diab, and shortly afterwards a dark group crowned the slope opposite the British camp, where a red tent was quickly pitched. A red tent is the sign of a king's residence in an Abyssinian army. In about half an hour the news was received that Kassai's main body, with drums beating and standards flying, was moving towards the Diab. In a short time the group of men round the tent was largely swollen, and soon about 4,000 soldiers could be made out on the summit of the hill. A few minutes before mid-day the army of Tigre began to advance down the slope towards the river. It numbered about 4,000 men, who moved steadily in a long deep line, to the music of rude kettledrums. Two yellow and red pendants, borne aloft in the centre, marked the position of the chief. As soon as the Abyssinians began to move, the British troops got under arms, and in a few minutes, from the opposite direction, were moving down towards the water. They halted about 100 yards from the stream, where a large tent had been erected for the meeting. The

British Commander-in-Chief mounted on an elephant, and, followed by his staff, rode down to the banks of the rivulet. The elephant was used on this occasion to impress Kassai, as the Abyssinians fear these animals much, and have never attempted to tame any of them. Close to the stream he dismounted from the larger animal, and mounted his horse, lest the approach of the huge earth-shaking beast should create a panic and cause disaster among the cavalry of Tigre. By this time the Abyssinian line was within 100 yards of the stream; it suddenly opened out in the centre, and Kassai, surrounded by his immediate counsellors and guard, rode forward on a white mule, with a crimson umbrella borne above his head. He forded the stream, and was received by Sir Robert Napier. Mutual salutations were exchanged, which, no doubt, were quite as sincere as those in daily vogue in the civilised world, although the words of each were quite unintelligible to the other. Kassai was then conducted to his tent, where he was received by a salute from a guard of honour. The unexpected rattle of the musketry blanched his cheek; doubtless a fear of treachery flashed through his mind. Then all dismounted, the British Commander led Kassai into the tent, and seating himself in a chair, placed Kassai in a chair on his right hand. Their respective officers ranged themselves on opposite sides of the tent—those of Kassai squatting on the floor, while those of Sir Robert Napier adhered to their more usual, although, perhaps, less natural, erect position.

Kassai was a young man of thirty-five years of age. His face, of a dark olive colour, was intellectual, but bore a careworn and wearied expression which justified the statement that he did not desire power, but that it was thrust upon him by the people of Tigre. He wore the Abyssinian costume, a white robe or toga embroidered with crimson, round his body, and the flowered silk shirt which marks those in high office round the king. His dark black hair was arranged in careful plaits which, drawn back from the forehead, were tied by a piece of riband round the back of the neck. The conversation was conducted through an interpreter. At first it consisted of almost meaningless enquiries after mutual health. But the Abyssinians soon threw out hints for presents of firearms. These hints were adroitly fenced, and the conversation turned to the subject of our mutual Christianity. In this subject neither the chief nor his followers appeared to take nearly so much interest as in that of the firearms, but they were held to it until it was suggested that a private interview would be desirable. The presents to be given to the Abyssinian chief were then brought in. They consisted of a double-barrelled rifle and some jugs and goblets of Bohemian glass. They were laid on the floor at Kassai's feet, and, after inspection, removed by one of his servants. The most valuable present of all could not be brought into the tent, but was surveyed through the doorway, as Sir Robert Napier gave to him a fine Arab horse which had been his own charger. The goblets were brought back for use, and port wine, which seemed much enjoyed by the Tigrean courtiers, was served out to them. According to Abyssinian custom the Commander-in-Chief had to drink some to prove that it was not a poison—a not unnecessary precaution, considering that it had been obtained from some spare hospital stores, as in a camp where all depended upon commissariat rations no wine could be obtained from any other source. The tent was then cleared of all but the Prince, the Commander-in-Chief, and two officers on either side, when serious matters were discussed.

Kassai was very anxious that the British army should undertake to guarantee his dominions against any invasion of his rival the Wagshum Gobaze. This Sir Robert Napier unhesitatingly refused, but promised that as far as advice and persuasion could go he would endeavour to secure peace between them; he also assured Kassai that he was sensible of the friendship of the people of Tigre during the passage of the army through that territory, and drew to his notice the fact that all supplies were honestly paid for, and that no native had cause of complaint for a blade of grass or an ounce of food taken wrongfully by either troops or followers. Kassai was also informed that plenty of supplies could be brought from the ships, but that the army would have to be longer in Tigre if no supplies could be found in the province, and he was requested to send grain to the posts at Adigerat and Antalo, being assured that if he did so it would be remembered in his favour when the British left the country, and that the Queen would reward him in some way which would please him.

Kassai was then left alone to rest, and about an hour later was summoned to witness a review of the British troops. The 3rd Bombay Light Cavalry, clad in light blue and silver; the 4th King's Own, in scarlet; the gunners of Murray's battery, in dark blue and red facings, and a small detachment of the 10th Native Infantry, with scarlet coats and white turbans, formed a picturesque and compact, though small force. The cavalry charged, the infantry skirmished and formed square, much to the admiration of the Abyssinians; but these were chiefly delighted and impressed by the Armstrong guns. Kassai dismounted and closely inspected the pieces, handled the shells, and looked through the rifled barrel, while some of his followers remarked that the English must be good Christians or Heaven would not grant them intelligence to mould such wondrous weapons. It appeared that to their view the greatest blessings which could be vouchsafed to Christian morality are firearms and gunpowder.

When the review was concluded, Sir Robert Napier

and the officers of his staff accompanied Kassai to the rivulet, and there intended to bid him farewell. At the point of parting, however, an urgent invitation was given that the English officers should visit the Abyssinian camp. The rivulet was crossed, and in a moment they found themselves in the middle of the army of Tigre. All were astonished at their appearance and armament. They clustered round the few Englishmen in dense but ordered masses. Their heads were bare, except for their plaited hair; their costumes were picturesque, long white togas embroidered with scarlet; they were nearly all possessed of firearms of every description, from the matchlock to the double-barrelled rifle, but by far the greater number had double-barrelled percussion guns of English or Belgian manufacture. Many had pistols, and all had the long crooked swords worn from the right side, a cut from which it is said to be impossible to guard. The few—but there were very few—not armed with firearms had the sword, spear, and shield. Of the four thousand now present, about four hundred were cavalry, mounted on mules or ragged wiry ponies. The horsemen were armed similarly to the foot soldiers. These men were truly an enemy not to be despised. Hardy mountaineers, quick in scaling the most difficult paths of their rugged country, they would give an infinity of trouble to any European force. Had Theodore's army been as well equipped, and more attached to their leader, much British blood might have been spilled before Magdála fell. Nor numerically were the soldiers of Tigre contemptible. At Adowa, his capital, Kassai had some six thousand more equally well armed. Their discipline was good, and in their short visit they showed a power of manœuvring which would not have disgraced the forces of a civilised nation. Their serious error was that at night no sentries or pickets were posted outside their camp. Hence the wonderful effect of Theodore's night attacks, for which he became famous, may be accounted for. He himself always adopted these necessary precautions.

Up the hill went the English staff with the drums beating in front of them, surrounded by dense clusters of wild warriors until they approached close to Kassai's tent. Here they dismounted and were bidden to enter. At the further side of the circular tent was a small couch covered with silk cloth on which the Prince took his seat, and placed Sir Robert Napier at his side. The Abyssinian officers of high grade sat round the tent on the floor at the left-hand side of their chief, while the English also seated themselves on the ground to the left of their commander. The scene was mixed and striking. The afternoon sun shone through the red tent, and lighted up with a crimson hue the robes and silken shirts of the Abyssinians and the uniforms of the Englishmen. Girls bearing large baskets of Abyssinian bread and curry came in and placed them on the ground in front of the visitors, who were requested to eat. The bread was brown, formed in flat circular cakes about a foot in diameter, and had a slightly sour taste. Very little sufficed to gratify curiosity, although it was permitted that each guest should help himself. In general, in Abyssinia, the servant, who brings in the loaves and curry, rolls some of the latter in a piece of the former, and after kneading it into a ball thrusts it into the mouth of each diner. After enough had been eaten, other girls entered bearing huge bullock horns filled with 'tedj,' a drink made from fermented honey. This 'tedj' or hydromel was poured into Florence flasks, one of which was given to each guest. It was expected that the recipient should bow towards the Prince and then empty his flask. No sooner, however, was the vessel emptied than it was seized by a watchful servant and again replenished. Each had to drink several flasks of the liquor, which tasted not unlike small beer, but rather sour. After a while, when many flasks had been emptied, musicians were introduced. The band consisted of six men who played on long pipes which uttered wild but not unpleasant music. A war song was then sung by a minstrel, and all the Abyssinians joined in chorus. The entertainment was now drawing to a close, and the presents were brought in which were to be bestowed upon the British Commander-in-Chief. He was first invested with a silver-gilt armlet, the sign of a great warrior. Then a lion's skin and mane, the mark of a fierce fighter in battle, were placed upon his shoulders, a sword was girt upon his side, and a spear and shield for him were handed to one of his staff who acted on the occasion as his armour-bearer. The meeting then broke up. Kassai, after frequent hand-shaking, accompanied the General to the door of the tent, where a grey mule caparisoned with Abyssinian saddlery and housings was waiting. On this Sir Robert Napier had to mount, and again accompanied by the Abyssinian army rode down to the Diab, where the Abyssinians halted. The English General and his staff rode into their own camp, but the shades of approaching night prevented the soldiery from witnessing the return of their leader in such an unwarlike guise.

Early the next morning Kassai paid a farewell visit to the British camp, and had a second private interview with Sir Robert Napier, at which he promised to afford security to convoys, and to threaten with severe punishment any who should endeavour to molest the telegraph through his dominions. He also promised to deliver weekly three thousand madrigals of wheat and barley, equivalent to about sixty thousand pounds, half at Adigerat and half at Antalo, for which he was to be paid. Such results of the interview were of no slight importance, for in a country where every man is a soldier, and a well-trained soldier, convoys would have to be most carefully guarded, posts well watched, strong and frequent garrisons maintained, and the line of telegraph continually patrolled if the population were hostile or even inclined to be unfriendly. Yet even the most sacred promises of the Prince of Tigre could not permit Sir Robert Napier to dispense with troops in position along the line of communication. The friendship of Kassai was of the utmost value; he was a chief over whose country the road of the army lay for above 150 miles, and whose refusal to allow the soldiers to have free access to wood and water would have involved a campaign in Tigre as a preliminary to the advance on Magdāla. Yet his friendship might prove fickle; he was young and newly seated on the throne, and he had several advisers who would have had him resent the entry of a foreign army into his dominions. His jealousy of Gobaze might rouse his anger against the English if they entered into friendship with the Wagshum, as they expected to be obliged to do, to secure similar advantages for the march through Lasta as the loyalty of Kassai would insure in Tigre. Even if Kassai meant and attempted to carry out his professions sincerely, it was open to doubt whether he had the power to prevent attacks being made upon the convoys. The petty chieftain of any small district, eager for plunder and careless of his prince's orders, might lead his clansmen to assault the convoys of stores in their passage from Senafe to the front. Thus, though it was probable that Sir Robert

Napier would gain something from his interview with Kassai, and the consequent friendship of the latter, and it was certain that at least a temporary quiet in the line of communications would be assured, his only real security was in being armed at all points, and in rendering himself, by his own judicious precautions, independent of all extraneous assistance.

On the 26th, at the same time as the red tent of Kassai was struck, and the army of Tigre disappeared from the opposite hill, the British column, under Sir Robert Napier, began its march towards Antalo. Passing by Adabagi, the line of fighting men, with their arms glittering in the bright sunlight, followed by the rumbling carriages of the artillery and a long crowd of transport mules, wound over some red sandstone hills, and in the afternoon plunged by a steep descent into the wide valley of the Dongolo river. Here, for the night, the camp was pitched beside the stream, the first which had yet been met with worthy of the name of river. The Mai Dongolo, or Dongolo water, which is enclosed between high banks overgrown with brushwood, is about thirty feet wide. There was not much water at the season when the army passed throughout all its course. It was only here and there in frequent pools that water was found, but where it was it was deep and good. Doubtless in rainy weather it would be a formidable obstacle. It crossed the route about 138 miles south of Adigerat.

The valley, about two miles broad, carpeted with long dry grass, is fenced in on either hand by high precipitous cliffs of red sandstone, which cast back with a lustrous glow the rays of the setting sun.

In the next day's march the character of the country entirely changed. The tabulated ranges of schistose mountain, and pinnacled crags of red sandstone, were left behind. The road instead now wound over large rolling hills of undulated limestone studded with acacia. The scenery was not unlike that of the South Downs, except that the hills were higher and larger, and instead of being clothed with short crisp grass, were rugged with detached stones, and showed only here and there much sign of herbage. Some of the masses of broken stone showed the presence of primeval corals in their formation, while nearly all were formed of densely compressed mussel and oyster shells, clearly visible to the naked eye. Ages ago they must have been deposited in the sea, when the mountainous highlands of Abyssinia lay in the bosom of the ocean and teemed with marine life. Some of the stones, when struck with a corresponding piece of rock, or even with a stick, returned a curious metallic ring. These are much prized in the country, and many of them, suspended by strings from the branches of trees in the churchyards, are used as bells to call the congregation to church. Interesting as these masses of rock might be to the geologist, they were great impediments to the march of the column. The infantry toiled through them tiresomely, the horses of the artillery strained hard upon the traces, and many a pack in the rough ground fell off some of the toiling baggage-animals, and had to be replaced by the rearguard, wearied with heat and dust. Had the soldiers of this detachment been consulted, the limestone formation would never have arisen from the bed of its natal ocean; or rather, perhaps, would now be undergoing metamorphic fusion in a temperature higher even than that of the Red Sea. None were sorry when, in a hollow, the banks of the Agula river were reached, where the night's camp was pitched. The day's march had been a short one, not ten miles, but painful, from the severe nature of the ground. By the banks of the Agula the site of a church was found, which had been built of square stones, and in a style of masonry high above the capabilities of the modern Abyssinians. It is supposed that it was constructed in the fourth or fifth century.

A still more toilsome journey than that of the previous day was performed on February 28. A high limestone down rose on the southern bank of the Agula: through a slight dip in this, called the Sallat Pass, the road was carried. The ground was of the same nature as on the previous day, but the march of fifteen miles was longer, and the ride up the Sallat Pass was a trying commencement. The guns of Murray's Battery, hauled by the horses and pushed by the gunners, accomplished the ascent, but not without difficulty; for though pioneers had been sent forward to make the road, they left but few marks of their labour behind them. Ridge after ridge had to be crossed. The horses of the artillery, wearied with incessant toil, and short of grain, had to be aided by working parties from the infantry, and at length, towards the afternoon, arrived at the banks of the Dolo river. The baggage animals suffered more. Unable to retain their footing on the slippery rock, many fell, and with difficulty regained their feet. All reached Dolo safely before the evening. One of the guns, indeed, broke a wheel, but was rescued from its difficulty by the aid of one of the two elephants which accompanied the force. At Dolo a halt was necessary, on the 29th, to rest the wearied troops, and the tired horses of the artillery. The following day the march recommenced, and Haik-Hellat river was reached. The route was not, however, carried through the village of that name, as it would have taken the army to the westward, off the direct line to the south. On this day (March 1), the advance-guard was at Musno, on the road between Antalo and Ashangi, about twenty-eight miles south of the Haik-Hellat; and Collings's brigade was at Buya, six miles south-east of Antalo, and troops were being closed up to the front from the rear as quickly as carriage became available.

On March 1, Sir Robert Napier left Dolo, and

marched to Haik-Hellat. The road lay over the Afgal range—a limestone ridge on the southern side of the Dolo river—and then descended sharply into the valley formed by the watercourse of Haik-Hellat. This valley, like most in this portion of Tigre, possessed a deep black soil, similar to that which is always found so favourable for the cultivation of cotton. At present these valleys are but little tilled; but if capital were invested upon them, and cotton grown, the country would soon become rich. The column of troops made the march easily, and on the following day reached the camp of Buya, which was situated about five miles and a half to the south-east of Antalo, and from its proximity to that town was generally known by the same name. Those who could obtain leave of absence did not march with the troops from Haik-Hellat to Buya, but, leaving them at the former place, turned to the west down the Haik-Hellat valley, and went to see the cathedral town of Chelicut. The road was steep and rocky, but the scenery amply repaid the toil of traversing it. The river, for a short distance, flowed clear as crystal, showing a bottom studded with many-coloured pebbles, over which the water bubbled, sparkling brightly in the hot morning sun. About a quarter of a mile below Haik-Hellat the stream fell, in a thin cascade about sixty feet in height, into a gorge, at the bottom of which it rolled sluggishly, under a dense canopy of reeds, rosebushes, myrtle, and corinda. The green foliage of these formed a striking contrast to the bare and rugged limestone crags that rose high on either hand, and were devoid of all vegetation, except occasional patches of tall dry grass. Down by the riverside ferns and water-plants sheltered in many a nook, and numerous acacias spread their slender boughs across the stream. These trees were thickly hung with bottle-shaped birds' nests, the numberless inhabitants of which sat among the branches sunning their dark-green plumage, or fluttered from twig to twig unconscious of danger. Three miles below Haik-Hellat the ravine opened out into a valley, and the town of Chelicut, built on the sloping mountain-sides, was reached. This place was far superior to any of the ordinary Abyssinian villages: the houses, instead of being constructed of mud and loose stones, were formed of neatly-squared masonry held together by cement. None were of more than one storey: some were circular, some square, but all had steep roofs thatched with the long grass which grew in the neighbouring part of the valley. Every house had its garden, in which vegetables of many kinds were cultivated. The potato, the French bean, maize, and peas could all be found in some one or other of the carefully-tended enclosures. The town contained about four hundred houses, the inhabitants of which poured forth in crowds, to stare at the strange white men who had come from some unknown far-off land to join in battle with the mighty Theodore. The men soon became quite friendly—partly from curiosity, partly from a desire to possess some of those countless dollars which popular Abyssinian rumour asserted every Frank to possess, and which a lucky fortune had directed to be scattered broadcast over Tigre. The women glanced slily at the strangers from behind doorways or over garden-walls, and when detected quickly started back, or covered up hastily their olive faces, leaving visible only a pair of dark sparkling eyes, which half invited, half repelled approach. Attended by a large crowd of men, all clothed in white togas trimmed with scarlet, and with no protection to their heads except their curly black hair, the visitors rode into the centre of the town, where, by the river-side, stood the cathedral, embosomed in a grove of lofty cypress-junipers. By the word 'cathedral' it must not be supposed that any massive pile of towering architecture was encircled by these trees. The church was but a circular building one storey high, roofed with thatch, and built in three concentric circles; the innermost, or most central, was the holy place, where the ark is kept, where priests alone may enter, and within which no strangers were admitted. The second had its walls ornamented with rude frescoes, which represented the Madonna and Child, the Crucifixion, the stoning of St. Stephen, and other incidents of New Testament history. The most prized of all was one of the Madonna encased in metal in Russian style, and a large fresco of St. George on a white horse killing the Dragon. None of the paintings were executed with the slightest regard to perspective, and seemed to be but rude imitations of the religious paintings of the early mediæval period. Into the second circle communicants are admitted. It was curious to find suspended on its walls, on either side of the reading-desk, two parchment scrolls in Tigrean character, one of which was headed with the British crown, the monogram 'G. R.,' and the words 'George King' in letters of gold. They must have been left there by Mr. Salt in one of his missions to Tigre in the earlier years of this century. The outer division of the church was but a colonnade; its walls were bare of either painting or ornament. In it the people pray, and prayers are publicly read. Several priests, distinguished from the laity only by wearing voluminous white turbans, showed the church, and explained the designs of the paintings, with frequent assertions that they were the work of native Abyssinian artists. At the door of the house of the Chief Priest they also exhibited the church plate. This consisted of a Bible bound in silver-gilt, two mitres of the same material manufactured by an Italian artist while resident in Abyssinia, a copper-gilt goblet with the arms of England and the motto 'Honi soit qui mal y pense,' a present from Mr. Salt, and a beautiful silver-gilt Greek cross, which many would willingly have purchased. While the Englishmen were inspecting these, they were themselves inspected. A thick crowd of the male inhabitants gathered round them, and examined with the greatest curiosity and admiration their swords, revolvers, watches, spurs, and clothing. Many, showing the blue beads round their neck which marked a Christian, asked by signs if the strangers were also Christians. On being assured that both professed the same faith, they ejaculated constantly, 'Tayeb,—tayeb!' the Arabic for 'good,' which the Abyssinians believed to be a word in the English language, and the British soldiers equally imagined to exist in that of Tigre, and which, with the exception of 'salaam,' was almost the only means of intercommunication between the two. After seeing and being seen as much as they considered necessary, the Englishmen remounted their horses and rode out of the town, accompanied past the outskirts of the houses by a whole host of newly-made friends, to the commencement of the open country, where they stopped and bade adieu, after receiving a present of some dollars for their church and the poor. A rough path across country, which left the town of Antalo situated on a rough plateau about halfway up the mountain called Amba Antalo, some two miles on the right, led to the camp at Buya.

Sir Robert Napier arrived on March 2 at this camp, which was in the immediate neighbourhood of Antalo, the halfway house between Zulla and Magdála. Here he caught up the brigade under General Collings, and halted with the main body of the troops until the 12th. The Pioneer Force was sent forward, and was strengthened: it now consisted of 200 sabres of the Sind Horse, under Major Briggs; 40 sabres of the 3rd Light Cavalry, under Colonel Loch; two companies of the 33rd Regiment, under Captain Trent; two companies of Beloochees, under Captain Hogg; one company of Punjab Pioneers, under Captain Currie; and the 3rd and 4th Companies of the Bombay Sappers, under Captain Goodfellow. These amounted, in all, to 280 cavalry and about 500 infantry, and were under the command of Brigadier Field. By direction of Colonel Phayre, they commenced, on March 4, to clear a road leading to Atalo by way of Mai Musgi Musno, and the defile of Gurubdek-dek; and in this labour they were occupied until the 9th, when a better and more direct route was discovered from Mai Musgi to Atalo by way of Meshik. Colonel Phayre had selected the longer route, from the bad accounts given of the shorter one by the natives at Mai Musgi. It was afterwards discovered that these reports had originated at the instigation of Walda Jasous, who held an *amba* on the shorter road, and did not wish the road to it opened up by the Pioneer Force. This report cost the Pioneer Force much useless toil. A few hours' ride, made by a staff-officer, might have saved much needless exertion and a considerable delay.

During the delay at Antalo, the Commander-in-Chief had, however, much to do. Antalo was the third post on the Abyssinian highlands, and here one of the main depôts was formed on the line of communication of which Senafe and Adigerat were the earlier links. To secure the stores which would be assembled there, the camp of Buya was surrounded by a stone wall, so traced as to admit of flanking defence.

At the camp of Buya, or Antalo—as it was more commonly called, from its proximity to that town—preparations were made for an advance in force towards the south. The army was redistributed in divisions, to each of which a separate duty was assigned. The First Division was composed of all troops which moved beyond Antalo; the Second Division of all troops which held the line of communication, and garrisoned the posts, between Antalo and the sea. The actual distribution ordered was as follows:—

HEAD-QUARTERS STAFF.

His Excellency Lieutenant-General Sir R. Napier, K.C.B., G.C.S.I., Commander-in-Chief.
Lieutenant-Colonel M. A. Dillon, Military Secretary.
Colonel the Hon. F. A. Thesiger, Deputy-Adjutant-General.
Captain T. J. Holland, Assistant-Quartermaster General.
Captain H. B. Pottinger, Deputy-Assistant-Quartermaster-General.
Major C. O. Maude, Deputy-Judge-Advocate-General.
Captain Hozier, Assistant Military Secretary.
Lieutenant R. Napier, Captain Scott, and Lord C. Hamilton, Aides-de-Camp.
Colonel Fraser, Commandant at head-quarters.
Brigadier-General Merewether, attached for Political duty.

Lieutenant Tweedie, Political Secretary.
Major Grant, C.B., Intelligence Department.
Captain Speedy, Intelligence Department.
Count Seckendoroff, His Prussian Majesty's Guards, Attached.
Captain Moore, Persian and Arabic Interpreter.

First Division.

All troops from Antalo to the front will compose the First Division.

Major-General Sir Charles Staveley, K.C.B., to command; Lieutenant-Colonel H. H. A. Wood, Assistant-Adjutant-General; Major H. Baigrie, Assistant-Quartermaster-General; Lieutenant Saunders, Aide-de-Camp.

Pioneer Force.

To march two days in advance of the First Brigade, First Division.

Brigadier-General Field, 10th Regiment Native Infantry, to command; Captain Durand, Brigade-Major; Captain MacGregor, Deputy-Assistant-Quartermaster-General; Lieutenant Shewell, Commissariat Officer; Captain Goodfellow, Field Engineer. Colonel Phayre, Deputy-Quartermaster-General, will accompany the Pioneer Force, and survey the road and country in its immediate neighbourhood.

Troops.—40 sabres 3rd Light Cavalry; 40 sabres 3rd Regiment Sind Horse; 3rd and 4th Companies Bombay Sappers and Miners; two companies 23rd Regiment Punjab Pioneers.

First Brigade, First Division.

Brigadier-General Schneider, to command; Captain Beville, Brigade-Major; Captain Hogg, Deputy-Assistant-Quartermaster-General; Major Mignon, Commissariat Officer.

Troops.—Head-quarters wing, 3rd Dragoon Guards; 3rd Regiment Light Cavalry; 3rd Regiment Sind Horse; G Battery 14th Brigade Royal Artillery, four guns; 'A' Battery 21st Brigade Royal Artillery; 4th King's Own Royal Regiment; head-quarters and eight companies 33rd Regiment; head-quarters 10th Company Royal Engineers; head-quarters and two companies 27th Regiment Native Infantry (Beloochees); head-quarters wing 10th Regiment Native Infantry.

Second Brigade, First Division.

Brigadier-General Wilby, to command; Captain Hicks, Brigade-Major; Captain Fawcett, Deputy-Assistant-Quartermaster-General; Major Barden, Commissariat Officer.

Troops.—Head-quarters wing 12th Bengal Cavalry; B Battery 21st Brigade Royal Artillery; two 8-inch mortars, with detachment 5-25 Royal Artillery; Rocket Battery Naval Brigade; K Company Madras Sappers and Miners; head-quarters and seven companies 23rd Regiment Punjab Pioneers; wing, 27th Regiment Native Infantry (Beloochees).

SECOND DIVISION.

Major-General G. Malcolm, C.B., Commanding; Major G. Bray, Assistant-Adjutant-General; Captain Watts, Deputy-Assistant-Quartermaster-General; Major Leven, Assistant-Commissary-General; Lieutenant Heath, Aide-de-Camp.

All troops at and from Senafe to Antalo will compose the Second Division.

ANTALO GARRISON.

Brigadier-General Collings, to command; Major Quin, Brigade-Major; Captain James, Deputy-Assistant-Quartermaster-General; Lieutenant Hore, Commissariat Officer.

Troops.—Wing 12th Bengal Cavalry; 5-25 Royal Artillery; H. Company Madras Sappers and Miners; 45th Foot; 3rd Regiment Native Infantry; detachment 10th Regiment Native Infantry.

ADIGERAT GARRISON.

Major Fairbrother, to command.

Troops.—Squadron 10th Bengal Cavalry; two guns, G 14, Royal Artillery; 2nd Company Bombay Sappers and Miners; wing 25th Regiment Native Infantry.

SENAFE GARRISON.

Lieutenant-Colonel Little, 25th Native Infantry, to command; Lieutenant Becke, 21st Native Infantry, Staff Officer; Captain Edwardes, Deputy-Assistant-Quartermaster-General; Commissariat Officer, Major Thacker.

Troops.—One squadron 10th Bengal Cavalry; 1st Company Native Artillery; three companies 21st Punjab Native Infantry; wing 10th Regiment Native Infantry; one company Marine Battalion; head-quarters wing 25th Regiment Native Infantry; depôts of all regiments in advance; 26th Cameronians (on arrival).

ZULLA COMMAND.

To be composed of all troops at Zulla and stations in the Passes. —Brigadier-General Stewart, to command; Brigade-Major, Captain Fellowes; Assistant-Quartermaster-General, Major Roberts; Deputy-Assistant-Quartermaster-General, Major Gammett; Commissariat Officer, Captain Hawkes.

Troops.—One squadron 10th Bengal Cavalry;·G Company Madras Sappers; 1st Company Bombay Sappers and Miners; 2nd Regiment

Native Infantry (Grenadiers); 18th Regiment Native Infantry; headquarters and five companies 21st Punjab Pioneers; 8th Bombay Native Infantry (on arrival); the 5th Bombay Native Infantry, to garrison stations in the Pass (on arrival).

The troops to compose the First Division who were not at Antalo were ordered up to the front. The 12th Bengal Cavalry, which reached Zulla on February 27, was directed to push up to Antalo by double marches, as were the 3rd Dragoon Guards, who disembarked on March 4. The 10th Bengal Cavalry was ordered to follow quickly. A detachment of the 5th Battery of the 25th Brigade of Royal Artillery, with forty elephants, two 8-inch mortars, and sixty-seven boxes of ammunition, the B Battery of 21st Brigade of Artillery, the 23rd Punjab Pioneers, the 45th Regiment, the Naval Brigade, and several companies of Sappers and Miners, were quickly moved, so that by the middle of March nearly all the troops which were to advance on Magdāla were around or in front of Antalo. All other preparations necessary for immediate operations were also made. Large working-parties from Zulla, consisting of the 2nd Grenadiers, the 18th Native Infantry, men of the Army Works corps, and the Cooley corps, were employed to push forward the railway. A second line of retreat was prepared, in case of accident to the Senafe Pass, by placing working-parties to improve the road through the Tekonda defile. The light engineer park, hospital trains, and hospital tents were brought forward, and a large amount of treasure was sent for to supply the means of purchasing food and animals in the country. The Highland Transport Train was largely supplemented by mules bought in the country, for which saddles and head-stalls had to be provided from the sea-coast; and the Transport Train found an auxiliary in the bullocks of the natives, which were freely hired to carry supplies along the line of communications, while the natives themselves, in considerable numbers and of both sexes, carried many loads.

CHAPTER VII.

ADVANCE TO ASHANGI.

ON March 12 Sir Robert Napier left Antalo and moved southwards. With him marched three troops of the 3rd Light Cavalry, 'A' Battery of the 21st Brigade Royal Artillery, the 10th Company Royal Engineers, the 4th (King's Own) Regiment, and two companies of Beloochees. The Commander-in-Chief moved by the more southern route, which leads by Amba Mayro and the Alaji Pass, 9,500 feet above the sea, to the Atalo valley, instead of by the one which had been so unfortunately selected by the reconnoitring department to waste the toil of the Pioneer Force in needless efforts to render the rugged Gurubdek-dek ravine and Musno hills passable for artillery. In this unnecessary task several days were consumed before the easier route by Amba Alaji was discovered; but as soon as it was, the Pioneer Force was diverted to its improvement. The troops which moved with the Commander-in-Chief halted at Meshik, where they remained for the following day, and assisted in clearing the route towards Musgi on the one hand and Atalo on the other. Sir Robert Napier himself, with a small escort of the 3rd Light Cavalry, made a double march to Atalo, where he came up with one portion of the Pioneer Force. Here he found the head-quarters and five companies of the 33rd Regiment, and two companies of the Punjab Pioneers. These troops were at once set to work to improve the roads. Orders were sent back to Antalo, that Murray's Armstrong battery of artillery should at once move to the front on elephants, escorted by a regiment of Native Infantry. On the following day (March 15), the Commander-in-Chief halted in his camp on the Atalo, and the troops quartered there were employed in clearing the route towards Makhan, over the steep hills near Amba Afagi. On this day Sir Charles Staveley marched into Atalo with the 'A' mountain battery, the 4th King's Own, the Beloochees, and the 3rd Light Cavalry.

The march from Meshik to Atalo lay over one of the great passes of the country, about 10,000 feet in height, above which scowled sullenly the almost inaccessible peak of Amba Afagi. The labour for baggage-animals was very heavy, but with good packing they managed to ascend and descend without so much difficulty as might have been expected. The troops had by this time, from constant practice, much improved in their method of adjusting the loads on the animals; but many of the pack-saddles were of a very indifferent pattern, and consisted solely of pads, across which the loads were slung in networks called 'selitas.' Some were not even supplied with means of securing the loads, and in going down steep descents, the weight was jerked forward on to the neck of the animal, which almost immediately fell. The incessant halts caused by the consequent delays were most vexatious, and the march was often so much delayed, that it was at last recognised that on such roads the infantry of the army could only be considered as a large baggage-guard. In consequence, Sir Charles Staveley adopted the system of distributing the regiments along the line of animals, and making each fighting man lead a mule. This reform was marked with success, for, though the track was steep, winding, and covered with loose stones, the march was accomplished in good time, and not a single load was left behind. Transport animals, unless provided with a driver apiece, are always under a great disadvantage in a rough country, from the necessity of tying them together in strings of three or four. Even with the most experienced and careful muleteers, this is a cause of much distress to the animals in passing over obstacles. The great advantage of a driver to each animal was amply demonstrated in Sir Charles Staveley's march to Atalo, as well as the freedom from falls or accidents of the mules which carried the batteries of 7-pounder mountain guns. On March 15 the Commander-in-Chief, who from this time assumed in person the direction of the Pioneer Force, marched with it from Atalo to Makhan, improving the road on the way. On arrival at the latter place, orders were sent back to Sir Charles Staveley to march the following day to Belago, and, halting there, to make the road practicable for the elephants which carried the mortars and Murray's guns. On the following day the Commander-in-Chief halted at Makhan, sending on five companies of the 33rd to Haya to make the road practicable for mules to that place. On the 17th, in accordance with his orders, Sir Charles Staveley moved with his first brigade from Atalo to Belago, five miles short of Makhan, and on the 18th pushed forward to Makhan. The Belago Pass was 9,700 feet above the sea.

The march from Atalo to Makhan, a distance of fifteen miles, was a very severe one, over a series of ascents and descents, which so sorely tried the baggage animals that many of those that accompanied the Pioneer Force broke down and had to be relieved of their loads, while a greater number did not arrive till the following morning, though they left Atalo very early in the day. A halt of the Pioneer Force was in consequence necessary for one day. Advantage of this was taken to re-arrange the postal duties between the front and Zulla. The mails were after this date carried by troopers of the 10th Bengal Cavalry, who were posted in small detachments along the whole line of communications. At the same time the transport for sick and wounded, which was to accompany the force beyond Antalo, was definitely decided upon; and it was arranged that doolies or dandies should be taken forward in the proportion of three to every hundred fighting men. On March 18 Sir Robert Napier, with the remainder of the Pioneer Force, marched to Ashangi. The last part of the road was found bad, but it was made practicable for mules by the Sappers and Pioneers as they marched. An order was sent back to Sir Charles Staveley to halt at Haya, and further improve the road, so as to render it practicable for elephants. Orders were also sent to Antalo for the head-quarters wing of the 10th Native Infantry to move to the front as soon as it was relieved by the 3rd Native Infantry, and on overtaking the elephants with the guns and mortars, to march with them as an escort. The head-quarters wing of the 45th Regiment and head-quarters wing of the 3rd Native Infantry were also ordered to move to the front as soon as possible. Reports came in from Zulla to say that animals and followers for the Transport Train were daily arriving; reports from the intermediate stations also told that the troops were quickly closing up to the front. The head-quarters and six companies of the 45th Regiment arrived at Senafe on March 13, escorting a convoy of 300,000 dollars and of 400 rounds of ammunition per man, and pushed forward the next morning towards Adigerat. The 3rd Regiment of Native Infantry arrived at Senafe on the 14th; two companies of Bombay Sappers and Miners reached Adigerat; and the head-quarters of the 12th Bengal Cavalry pushed forward from the same place on that day. The 23rd Punjab Pioneers, 485 strong, and the Naval Brigade arrived at Antalo on the 16th, and on the 17th pushed forward with a detachment of Sind Horse, the B battery of the 21st Brigade of Royal Artillery, and the left wing of the 33rd Regiment, which mustered 325 men. On the same day there arrived at Antalo small detachments of the 12th Bengal Cavalry, of the 3rd Light Cavalry, of the Sind Horse and of the Royal Engineers, as well as the Engineer Park.

The route from Makhan to Lake Ashangi lay round the edge of a mountain range covered with juniper trees which formed a thick jungle. The path itself was irregular and winding. After crossing a deep valley a summit was gained at an elevation of 9,400 feet, whence the first view of Lake Ashangi could be obtained. Much had been told of this lake, and it was expected to be a wide sheet of water. Such was not the case, as it was only about four miles long and three broad, but it was surrounded by noble hills which enclosed besides the lake a luxuriant and fertile valley, covered with waving crops of standing corn, while numerous villages were clustered on the hillsides, as if sentinels of the fertility beneath them. The uninhabited borders of the lake were treacherous and deceitful, being nearly everywhere morasses, into which men sank without notice, and where more than one sportsman, too intent upon his game, sank down, and with difficulty escaped being suffocated.

The villages in the vicinity of Lake Ashangi are perched on high conical rocks, or in elevated situations on the hill-sides, and are surrounded by fences of 'kolqual,' to defend them from the attacks of the Azebo Gallas, who live not far off, are professors of the Mahommedan faith, and are bound by the laws of their tribe to kill a Christian before they can take a wife. Bloodshed is common in this district, and some stragglers from the army suffered at the hands of the Gallas, but probably more on account of their own carelessness in violating the susceptibilities of these people, than because of any desire of the Gallas to enter into hostilities with the British troops.

CHAPTER VIII.

ADVANCE TO LAT.

ON March 20, Sir Robert Napier with the main body of the Pioneer Force marched from Lake Ashangi over the plain of Wofela to the camping ground of the Mesagita. The distance was short—not more than seven miles—and the road was not bad according to Abyssinian estimate, except for the first few hundred yards. The pass, nearly 10,000 feet high, beyond Mesagita leading over the Womberat chain of hills to Lat, was reported to be very difficult; therefore two companies of the Pioneers and two companies of Bombay Sappers were marched forward on the 20th to improve it, and the Commander-in-Chief halted on the 21st at Mesagita, sending forward a wing of the 33rd Regiment to assist them in their labours. On the 22nd the A battery of the 21st brigade of Royal Artillery, and four companies of Beloochees, under Sir Charles Staveley, Colonel Milward, and Colonel Penn, marched in one day from Ashangi, and joined the Commander-in-Chief at Lat. Here arrangements were made to complete the Highland Transport Train to a strength of 8,000 mules south of Antalo. This highland train was exceedingly successful. It was organised on much the same principles as had been originally proposed by the Commander-in-Chief for the whole transport of the Abyssinian expedition—a proposal unfortunately not accepted. It consisted nominally of four divisions; each division consisted numerically of 2,000 mules, and as at Lat measures were adopted for striking sick and non-effective animals off the muster-rolls, and placing them in stationary hospitals or depôts along the line of communications, in the further advance the highland train did actually count 8,000 mules. To each division were attached one captain and three subalterns, while the whole was under the command of Captain Hand of the 82nd Regiment, who was responsible to the Commander-in-Chief alone, and received the orders of the latter through the officer at head-quarters, who performed the duties of quartermaster-general. Three permanent staff officers were attached to the train, one of whom worked under Captain Hand at head-quarters, one was stationed at Antalo, and one at Adigerat. It was the duty of these officers to supervise the gear, the arrangement of convoys, the hospitals and depôts, and to replace mules who arrived sick, footsore, or galled, by sound ones from the depôts at their disposal. There was besides an inspector of the Transport Train, who continually passed up and down the line from station to station, took care that the proper arrangements were properly carried out, and reported daily confidentially to the Commander-in-Chief. By this time also the muleteers who had been despatched from Persia, Syria, and Egypt had been almost entirely replaced by natives of India, who could understand and be understood by their officers and by each other. A considerable proportion of the new muleteers were Punjabees who had acquired experience in the mule trains of Lahore and Rawul Pindee, and were disciplined and armed, while for the others native arms were bought, which placed them on equality at least with the Abyssinians. It was derived from the experience of this campaign that it is of great importance that the drivers of a land transport train should be sufficiently under discipline and control to be trusted with arms, as they are then enabled to dispense to a great extent with escorts, especially when the animals are sent out to graze, and the sidearms are also available for cutting grass.

At Lat, new arrangements were made for the distribution of the troops, and it was ordered that the troops of the Pioneer Force, and of the 1st and 2nd Brigades, should proceed without baggage: in consequence of which the following General Orders were issued.

The following distribution of troops in the 1st or Sir C. Staveley's Division, is ordered:—

First Brigade.

Brigadier-General Schneider; Captain Beville, Brigade-Major; Captain Hogg, Deputy-Assistant-Quartermaster-General; Captain Goodfellow, Field Engineer.

Troops. — Head-quarters, 3rd Sind Horse ; A-21 Steel Battery ; 1st Battalion 4th (King's Own) Royal Regiment; Head-quarters and six companies 23rd Punjab Pioneers ; 10th Company Royal Engineers ; Head-quarters wing, 27th Native Infantry.

SECOND BRIGADE.

Brigadier-General Wilby; Captain Hicks, Brigade-Major; Captain James, Deputy-Assistant-Quartermaster-General.

Troops.—Head-quarters, 3rd Light Cavalry ; B-21 Steel Battery Naval Rocket Brigade; 33rd (Duke of Wellington's Regiment).

THIRD BRIGADE.*

Brigadier-General Field ; Captain Durant, Brigade-Major ; Captain Edwards, Deputy-Assistant-Quartermaster-General ; Lieutenant Jopp, Assistant Field Engineer.

Troops.—Four guns G-14 Royal Artillery ; Nos. 3 and 4 Companies Bombay Sappers and Miners ; two companies Punjab Pioneers; two 8-inch mortars of 5-25 Royal Artillery ; K Company Madras Sappers and Miners ; one company of the 33rd Foot, and a company of the 4th Foot, who will hereafter rejoin their corps when the Brigade is well advanced to the front.

The following distribution of officers of the 1st Brigade was ordered :—

Sind Horse.—One tent for regimental officers and the two officers attached.

Royal Artillery Head-quarters and the First Division.—One tent for Colonel Petrie, Captain Geary, Lieutenant-Colonel Milward, Captain Nolan, and the officers of A-21 Royal Artillery.

33rd Foot.—Two tents for regimental officers, Dr. Austen and Major Leveson.

23rd Pioneers and Beloochees.—One tent for regimental officers, Messrs. Henty, Stanley, and Whiteside.

10th Company Royal Engineers and Land Transport Train.—One tent for regimental officers, Lieutenant Shewell, Mr. Holmes, and Mr. Sheppard.

Head-quarters and Personal Staff.—One tent.

Intelligence Department.—One tent for General Merewether, C.B., Lieutenant Lockhart, Mr. Markham, and Lieutenant Tweedie.

No mule will be loaded except by bugle sound, which will sound a

---

* This Brigade will be employed in making the road onward to Magdāla practicable for laden elephants, and will join the 1st and 2nd Brigades as soon as that work has been accomplished.

quarter of an hour before the hour of march. On the sound of the bugle every mule will be tightly girthed before being loaded. Great care must be taken to see that the breast straps and breechings are properly adjusted.

The following troops *en route* to the front on reaching the 3rd Brigade will be passed on to join the 1st and 2nd Brigades under the above-mentioned regulations:—Head-quarters 3rd Dragoon Guards; head-quarters 10th Cavalry; wing, 45th Foot; wing, 3rd Native Infantry; wing, 27th Native Infantry; head-quarters and one company Bombay Sappers and Miners.

The kits of the officers, non-commissioned officers, and rank and file will be left behind to be brought on by the 3rd Brigade.

Arrangements will be made by the Brigadier-General Commanding for their safe custody and safe transport to the front.

Tents will be allowed in the proportion of one to every twelve officers, and one to every twenty non-commissioned and rank and file.

Major-Generals commanding divisions will be allowed one tent.

Brigadier-Generals will be allowed one tent for themselves and for their personal and brigade staff.

Hospital tents will be allowed to such regiment, battery, or detachment, according to recommendation of principal medical officer; with that exception no other tents must be taken for any other purpose whatever.

The 23rd and Beloochees will take entrenching tools sufficient for one company each.

A light hospital establishment to accompany each detachment.

All sick men and horses will be left behind to be brought up by the 3rd Brigade.

Fifteen days' rations according to the following scale will be carried by each detachment and battery:—

EUROPEANS.		NATIVES.	
Biscuit or flour	1 lb.	Flour	1 lb.
Vegetables	2 oz.	Ghee, if purchased locally	2 oz.
Sugar	1½ ,,	Salt	½ ,,
Tea	½ ,,	Vegetables once a week	2 ,,
Rum	1 dram.		

The Commissariat will take in sufficient rice to meet casual demands, and will make arrangements for rationing staff officers and their followers.

Officers will be allowed to take on any riding animals they may have in their possession, but their loads must be limited to the officers' own bedding and their horses' kit.

No private baggage animals or camp equipage will be allowed to follow the column under any pretext whatever.

Carriage will be allowed for cooking pots of officers in the proportion of one mule to every twelve officers.

No baggage mule proceeding with the force will carry more than 100 lbs.; except in the case of bearers of small-arm ammunition and tents, when two of each will be the load: 4 lbs of grain will be carried, in addition to the 100 lbs., to complete the day's ration.

Officers in charge of the commissariat must make up the weight of their ration bags, rum kegs, and vegetable boxes to 50 lbs. each.

The cooking pots of batteries and detachments will be carried in the proportion of 50 lbs. to each company or troop.

British troops will march in serge or Khakee clothing according to Brigade arrangements (the suit of clothing which is not worn will be carried for the soldier), and will carry one blanket and a waterproof sheet in addition to the great coat and canteen.

Officers who do not possess a riding animal will have two blankets and a waterproof sheet carried for each, under regimental arrangements. This also applies to Native officers.

All records, company's books, &c., will be left behind to come on with the 3rd Brigade.

Sick carriage will be taken on in the full proportion as at present allowed.

All doolies, however, will be brought on in the rear of the whole baggage of the brigade.

Small-arm ammunition will be carried in saluters or Bombay saddles.

One man, inclusive of muleteers, will be told off to every mule to lead him during the march: should any load require readjusting, assistance will be given him by the man in rear, and on no account must the mules in front be stopped.

It was from Lat that the real rapid advance on Magdāla began. Up to this point the Commander-in-Chief had been merely making his steady preparations, which enabled him to swoop swiftly down upon his adversary and seize his prey. Before leaving Lat, he received a report from Senafe to say that the five companies of the 25th Native Infantry had left that place on March 16, for the front, escorting the first reserve ammunition of A-21, B-21, and G-14 Batteries Royal Artillery, as well as thirty mule-loads of hospital stores, and twenty mule-loads of telegraph stores. It was also reported from Antalo that on March 18 there left that place for the front four Armstrong guns of G-14 Battery Royal Artillery, two 8-inch mortars, K Company of Sappers, the head-quarters of the 12th Bengal Cavalry, and Brigadier-Generals Schneider and Wilby.

CHAPTER IX.

ADVANCE TO THE TAKKAZIE.

ON March 23 Sir Robert Napier advanced from Lat to Marawa with the head-quarters and five companies of the 33rd Regiment; the head-quarters and four companies of the Beloochees; A Battery 21st Brigade Royal Artillery, and the head-quarters and three troops of the Sind Horse.

Sir Charles Staveley with his force removed to Lat. Reports were received at Marawa which told that G battery of the 14th Brigade Royal Artillery, two 8-inch mortars, a wing of the 12th Bengal Cavalry, and the Engineer Park, arrived at Atalo on March 20, from the same place; a difficulty in obtaining native carriage was also reported, and Captain Moore of the Intelligence Department was sent back to arrange it. Reports were also received from Adigerat which told that the head-quarters and six companies of the 45th Regiment arrived at that place on the 17th, and pushed forward on the 18th. The head-quarters and right wing of the 3rd Native Infantry also arrived at Adigerat on the 18th, having made a double march from Goona-goona.

Notwithstanding the reduction of baggage, the road was so bad between Lat and Marawa that although the distance was only eleven miles, it was considered fortunate that all the mules of the Transport Train reached the latter place before dark. The road along which the army slowly toiled and clambered incessantly over mountain after mountain was so narrow that any halt or break-down in the column made every man and animal in its rear pause. Daily it became more apparent, how impracticable had been the suggestions of those who had advocated from the outset a dash upon Magdála.* To diverge from the path was out of the question, as it ran along the side of steep sandstone hills, with a precipice below, and the densely-wooded hill-face rising abruptly above. On the following day the Commander-in-Chief moved from Marawa to Dildi. It had been anticipated that the nature of the road would prevent rapid progress;

* The able special correspondent of the *Times* wrote thus on this march:—'No caricaturist would, I hope, have the heart to make fun of us and our expedition, considering how much trouble we are taking, and upon what a hopeless task we are engaged. But could such a man be found, it must, I fear, be admitted that our "dash" upon Magdála would present him with a very tempting picture. If incongruity be the essence of humour, he ought to make any amount of capital out of the contrast between all that is associated with the word "dash" and our long line of horses, mules, and bullocks, toiling at the rate of about a mile and a half an hour over a series of almost perpendicular ascents and descents— tumbling backwards, forwards, sideways—now and then bringing the "dash" to a dead halt by choking the way in one helpless palpitating mass of heads, tails, and shoulders, merely because a weak or cantankerous brother in the front refuses to move on.'

therefore the first start was made at a very early hour, and every quarter of an hour groups of baggage animals were despatched, until the whole were well on their way by nine o'clock. The nature and length of the road far exceeded, however, the worst anticipations. The first few miles were passed without great difficulty, as the army followed a route originally constructed by Wagshum Gobaze. Parts of the road were as difficult as that through the Sooro Pass before any labour had been expended upon it. It was rugged, devious, and broken, and before some of the animals had cleared half of the distance, the sun was already declining. Thunder had been heard in the surrounding hills during the afternoon, and towards evening a terrific storm broke upon the line of march. Night soon came on, and the rear of the column was surprised by pitchy darkness. It was, however, impossible to halt; the troops were forced to push on, and the last, the Beloochees, reached the camp of Dildi late in the evening. The commissariat train did not however come in till the following morning. The march was one of unprecedented severity in the war; every soldier carried fifty-five pounds, including his ammunition. All were drenched by the thunderstorm, and had no change of clothes. The tents of many did not arrive till next morning, and, wet and weary, they had to pass the night on the slushy ground.

After the severe march of the preceding day, a halt

was made at Dildi, to refresh the troops. Here much information of Theodore's movements, but little on which reliance could be placed, was received by means of spies. Some asserted that he was preparing for the defence of Islamgi; others that he meant to fight on the Bashilo; others that he would make a night attack on the British force as soon as it had reached the Dalanta plateau. Little credit was given to the last assertion; but no precautions were neglected, and the vedettes and picquets were doubled. At Dildi, some supplies of fowls and eggs, which were exceedingly grateful, were obtained from the people of the country, and here a depôt was established.

After a day's halt at Dildi the Commander-in-chief with the 1st Brigade, to which now the 4th (King's Own) Regiment was attached instead of the 33rd, moved to Wondaj, followed at the interval of one march by Sir Charles Staveley with the 2nd Brigade, who was again followed at a similar interval by the 3rd Brigade, with the elephants and heavy artillery. At Wondaj the force was again exposed to a terrific thunderstorm just as it reached its camping ground, which being ploughed land was quickly converted into a muddy quagmire. The distance was not, however, more than seven miles; and a continuous ascent of 3,000 feet brought the force to the head of the Wondaj Pass, 10,500 feet above the sea; whence there was a grand view of the Valley of the Takkazie, bounded on the south by the hills of Santara. On the following day, the 27th, the advance was continued to Moja, another distance of about seven miles On the night that the 1st Brigade halted at Moja the camp was thrown into considerable excitement by the arrival of an officer with a letter from Colonel Phayre, who was reconnoitring with some horsemen a few miles ahead, which said that Mr. Munzinger, who had been sent to open communication with Wagshum Gobaze, was missing, and had doubtless fallen into the hands of Theodore, while Theodore himself had crossed the Bashilo, and was advancing to defend the passages of the Takkazie. This information subsequently was discovered to be without foundation; but Sir Robert Napier was determined that he would next day secure the passage of the Takkazie and the steep ascent beyond it to the Wadela plateau, in case Theodore might seek to take advantage of the favourable defensive position which the summit of the abrupt southern bank of the Takkazie would afford him. On the following morning, accordingly, the force moved down from Moja to the Takkazie, where measures had been taken for the collection of grain to feed the animals, which were here unloaded and permitted to rest, while strong working parties of the 4th, the Beloochees, and the Punjabees were pushed forward, under Captains Goodfellow and Le Mesurier, to form a practicable path up the steep and precipitous southern bank of the Takkazie, which rose abruptly above the river to a height of more than 4,000 feet. After no great length of time, a sapper on the summit signalled that the road was prepared, and the force began to climb the steep ascent. Not without difficulty it crowned the summit, but before dark it did so, and the passage of the Takkazie was secure for the whole of the army. That night the Commander-in-Chief halted on the river Santara, sending back word to Sir Charles Staveley to push on and concentrate with him. The Takkazie, in March, was anything but a formidable river; it was, in fact, but a series of pools, yet in the rainy season it must be a magnificent mass of water, as it is the principal tributary of the Blue Nile, which sweeps down the rich soil of Abyssinia to fertilise the valley of Egypt.

CHAPTER X.

ADVANCE TO THE BASHILO.

ON account of the difficulty in regard to native carriage, the 1st Brigade arrived at Santara on the 28th, and halted there for two days, where Sir Robert Napier received a visit from the uncle of Wagshum Gobaze, who arrived with a body of 400 cavalry, which raised the estimate of the Abyssinian horse in the eyes of the Europeans. Wagshum Gobaze himself wrote to Sir Robert Napier, expressing his regret that they could not have a personal interview, as he was necessarily absent in Begemder; but his uncle and emissary, Mashesha, stated that he had instructions to render to the British all the aid in his power. On the morning of the 30th, the 2nd Brigade, under Sir Charles Staveley, marched into Santara. Here the 3rd Brigade was broken up, and amalgamated with the 1st and 2nd Brigades; and Colonel Field, its brigadier, reverted to the command of the 10th Native Infantry.

Santara, where the Commander-in-Chief halted for two days, to concentrate the 1st and 2nd Brigades, is on the edge of the table-land of Wadela, which has an average height of 11,500 feet above the sea level. The climate here and on the plateau was very variable; in the daytime the thermometer stood about 75 degrees, at night it fell to 19½ degrees, and ice was sometimes formed in a closed tent with four or five occupants. Between the Takkazie and the Bashilo, besides the Wadela plateau, lie the two plateaux of Dalanta and Daunt, south of the Bashilo; and in the fork formed between that river and one of its tributaries, the Kulkulla, is huddled together the knot of mountains of which Magdāla is the key. In order to reach this fortress of King Theodore, the route of the army lay across the intervening plateaux of Wadela and Dalanta. The formation of both of these is basaltic, and they are consequently intersected by steep and precipitous ravines. In the most important of these, which separates the highland of Wadela from that of Dalanta, runs the river Jidda.

Apparently the most easy route of approach to the Bashilo from Santara would have been round the upper sources of the Jidda, by a place called Kosso Amba; but the various information which could be obtained, as well as the able reports of Mr. Munzinger —who had been despatched by Sir Robert Napier to visit Wagshum Gobaze, and had taken the opportunity to reconnoitre the country—told that the ground about Kosso Amba was much broken and that the most advantageous way for the march to be conducted would be in a south-westerly direction, along the Wadela plateau, to a place called Bethor, on the edge of the Jidda ravine, where the road which Theodore had constructed, on his march from Debra Tabor to Magdála, for the passage of his heavy baggage and big mortars, dipped into the defile of the Jidda. From this point, advantage could be taken of Theodore's own road to advance against him at Magdála. On March 31, accordingly, the 1st Brigade moved from Santara to Gaso, and on April 1 from Gaso to Abdakom, followed by the 2nd Brigade, which halted on April 1 at Gaso.*

* On April 1 the whole British force in Abyssinia consisted of 10,800 fighting-men, with 14,500 followers, who were attached to the Land Transport Train, Commissariat Department, Regiments, &c. Its distribution was as follows:—

The head-quarters, with Brigadier-General Schneider's 1st Brigade of the 1st division, consisting of the following troops, at Abdakom:—

3rd Regiment Sind Horse	208
Head-quarter wing 12th Bengal Cavalry	150
Naval Brigade Rocket Battery.	83
A Battery 21st Brigade R.A. (steel 7-pounder guns)	122
Head-quarters 10th Company R.E.	32
4th King's Own Royal Regiment	530
23rd Regiment Punjab Pioneers	671
Head-quarters wing 27th N.I. (Beloochees)	327
	2,123

The head-quarters of the 1st division, under the command of Major-General Sir Charles Staveley, with the 2nd Brigade, under Brigadier-General Wilby, at Gaso, one march in rear of the head-quarters of the army and of the 1st Brigade:—

TROOPS.

Head-quarters and four troops 3rd Bombay Light Cavalry	171
G Battery 14th Brigade R.A. (four 12-pounder Armstrong guns)	92
Detachment 5/25 R.A., with two 8-inch mortars	35
B Battery 21st Brigade R.A. (steel 7-pounder guns)	109
Head-quarters and K Company Madras Sappers and Miners	131
Head-quarters and 2nd, 3rd, and 4th Companies Bombay Sappers and Miners	294
33rd (Duke of Wellington's) Regiment	700
Head-quarters wing 10th Regiment N.I.	217
	1,749

The halt at Santara was not entirely caused by the necessity of concentration of the 1st and 2nd Bri-

The following troops were *en route* to join the 1st and 2nd Brigades, 1st division, and were on this date at the following stations:—

Head-quarters and six companies 45th Regiment, at Waulaj, two marches in rear of 2nd Brigade	385
Head-quarters wing 3rd Regiment N.I. at Dildi	300
One troop 3rd Light Cavalry at Dildi	73
Wing 27th N.I. Regiment (Beloochees) at Marawa	286
Head-quarters wing 3rd Dragoon Guards at Makhan	220
Head-quarters squadron 10th Bengal Cavalry, on the march from Antalo	140
	1,404

The 1st division left all baggage and stores at Lat: this baggage had since been brought on to Dildi, and the stores at that place were left under the charge of a guard of fifty dismounted men of the 3rd Regiment of Sind Horse. All troops in advance of Dildi were marching without baggage, and with a limited supply of bell-tents, sufficient to accommodate twelve officers, or twenty non-commissioned officers and rank and file each. Each regiment carried with it rations for fifteen days. The loads on the mules had been reduced to 100 lbs. each, to enable them to move easily, and the troops carried their greatcoats, blankets, and waterproof sheets on their backs, in addition to their accoutrements and sixty rounds of ammunition. Officers not mounted had a greatcoat, blanket, and waterproof sheet carried for them. A detachment of 130 men of the 10th Regiment of Native Infantry was at Atalo, escorting stores to the front: detachments, consisting of one duffedar and twelve men of the 3rd and 12th Cavalry, were at each postal station from Antalo to Lat, and parties of one duffedar and six men at each station from Lat to the front.

The troops comprising the 2nd division of the force, under the command of Major-General Malcolm, C.B., were stationed at Antalo, Adigerat, and Senafe, were as follows:

At Antalo, Brigadier-General Collings commanding:—

1 troop 3rd Bombay Cavalry	73
1 company Bombay Sappers and Miners	126
Wing 3rd Regiment Native Infantry	375

The following troops had been ordered up, and were *en route* to Antalo, to join the garrison of that station:—

5/25 Battery Royal Artillery, with 6-pounder brass guns	90
4 companies 45th Regiment	280
3 companies 25th Regiment Native Infantry	190

gades, but on account of the delay in arrival of provisions. No flour could be obtained in Wadela, and the army was dependent on its chain of communications and on its carriage. On March 31, General Merewether was sent back to the Takkazie, to arrange some difficulties with the owners of native bullocks

At Adigerat:
1 troop 12th Bengal Cavalry	70
2 12-pounder Armstrong guns of G Battery 14th Brigade R.A.	60
Head-quarters and 5 companies 25th Regiment N.I.	430

At Senafe:
1 troop 10th Bengal Cavalry	73
No. 1 Company Native Artillery, with Mountain Train	60
Wing 10th Regiment Native Infantry	337
3 companies 21st Punjab Native Infantry	240
1 company 21st Bombay Native Infantry (Marine Battalion)	87

Detachments of one duffedar and twelve men of the 10th and 12th Bengal Cavalry were located at each postal station between Senafe and Antalo; and fifty men of the 12th Bengal Cavalry were at Agula, halfway between Antalo and Adigerat, and small detachments of cavalry and native infantry were at such stations between Senafe and Antalo as were considered advisable by the General Officer commanding the division. The 26th Regiment (Cameronians) embarked at Vingorla on March 17, and were ordered, on arrival, to move from Zulla, to supplement the garrisons of Senafe and Adigerat.

The Zulla brigade was under the command of Major-General Russell, and consisted of the following troops stationed at Zulla, and the different stations in the pass between Zulla and Senafe:—

At Zulla, 18th Regiment Bombay Native Infantry	680
,, Komayli, 2nd Regiment Bombay Native Infantry	702
,, Sooro, 2 companies 21st Punjab Native Infantry	160
,, Undul Wells, head-quarters and 2 companies 21st Punjab Native Infantry	160
,, Raha Guddy, 1 company 27th Punjab Native Infantry	80

The Zulla command was to have been strengthened by the 5th and 8th Regiments of Bombay Native Infantry, but they did not arrive till after the fall of Magdāla, and never disembarked.

employed in the transport of provisions, and the settlement of similar difficulties near Atalo was entrusted to Major Grant and Captain Moore.

All precautions were taken against a night-attack by Theodore on the road across Wadela. It was well known that he had many spies, who daily reported to him the British movements, and in the Wadela plateau several horsemen were seen, who could be easily recognised to be scouts, but were too astute to allow themselves to be captured by our cavalry. The picquets and vedettes were nightly posted by Colonel Fraser, V.C., of the 11th Hussars, who had been appointed Commandant of Outposts, and were frequently and minutely inspected.

Near Gaso an abundance of hornblendic rock was found, which had the outward appearance of coal, and, as fuel was scarce, was eagerly seized upon by the soldiers to cook with. It was quickly discovered, however, upon trial, to be incapable of sustaining combustion.

Conventions, with the native proprietors of transport animals, were made at Abdakom for the carriage of supplies from the Takkazie to Bethor.

On April 2 the Commander-in-Chief, with the 1st Brigade, moved his camp from Abdakom, a distance of about two miles, to Yesendie, and Sir Charles Staveley moved from Gaso to Abdakom, so that the force was concentrated in case of attack. Here there occurred an incident which might have been attended with serious consequences. Mashesha, the uncle of the Wagshum Gobaze, again paid a visit to Sir Robert Napier with about 200 followers, and when his visit was concluded, he was escorted by an officer beyond the outposts of the 1st Brigade. On his way to a neighbouring village, he used a road which led close past one of the outposts of Staveley's brigade, where a corporal and four men of the 3rd Light Cavalry were stationed. This picquet was totally unaware that the body of Abyssinian cavalry had come from the camp of the 1st Brigade, and warned the horsemen not to approach. The latter replied with shouts of derision, brandishing their lances. The corporal, presuming that they were a detachment of Theodore's cavalry, ordered one of his party to fire, and the shot was returned: the remainder of the picquet then fired and advanced against the natives, who retreated, but with the loss of one killed and one wounded. At the sound of the shots the troops stood to their arms, but it was soon discovered that the affair originated in a mistake. Mr. Munzinger was despatched to the Abyssinian camp, to explain the matter, and offer a pecuniary compensation to the relatives of the killed. The compensation and apology were readily accepted, and any serious complications with the Wagshum happily averted.

On April 4, Sir Robert Napier broke up his camp

at Yesendie, and moved across the ravine of the Jidda to the Dalanta plateau. The Punjab Pioneers, the A Battery of the 21st Brigade Royal Artillery, and two companies of the 4th (King's Own) Regiment, under the command of Colonel Milward, R.A., had marched from Yesendie, on the afternoon of the 3rd, to clear the road down to the Jidda river, with orders to move upon Avercot early on the morning of the 4th, and secure the summit of the ascent from the Jidda defile. On the morning of the 4th, Colonel Milward ascended from the Jidda, and seized the entrance on to the Dalanta plateau. The Commander-in-Chief, with the 1st Brigade, followed closely to support the advanced guard; while the 2nd Brigade, under Sir Charles Staveley, occupied Bethor, and closed down to the edge of the ravine.

At Bethor the British force struck the road constructed by Theodore on his march from Debra Tabor to Magdála, for the transport of his heavy ordnance, and moved across the Jidda on the very track left by the Negoos. At Bethor, and across the Dalanta plateau, could be constantly seen the vestiges of Abyssinian camps, and the ruins of the huts in which the troops of the Emperor had dwelt. He had been at that place on January 1; the British army occupied it on April 3, but Theodore's progress had been slow: it was but on the 28th of the same month that he reached the banks of the Jidda, on February 5 that he reached Avercot, and on March 1 that he commenced his descent into the ravine of the Bashilo. On March 14 he crossed that river, on the 18th halted at Arogi, and on the 25th took up his position at Islamgi, where his camp could be seen by the British on the Dalanta plateau on April 5.

The difficulty of the march between Yesendie and Avercot consisted in the descent and ascent of the Jidda ravine, the bottom of which lay at a depth of three thousand feet below the table-land of the conterminous plateaux. Eighteen miles lay between the camps occupied by the Commander-in-Chief on the night of the 4th and 5th April, of which eleven were within the banks of the Jidda, and nine either sharp descent or ascent. As the army approached the ravine, other traces of Theodore also became apparent. The stubble and hay which had before covered the country were burnt, and the ground was covered with ashes; no flocks or herds were to be seen, and scarcely a single human being could be found. In place of farm-houses and villages, there were but ruined heaps of blackened stones. The road, which had been constructed by the author of this desolation, was a grand feat of rude engineering; rocks had been hurled aside or blasted through, at an immense expense of labour and of time; the gradient was uniform but very steep, and the broad roadway was covered with loose stones, which had obviously been employed to prevent his heavy ordnance from running too rapidly down the slope. It was not without toil that the march was accomplished; the leading companies did not reach their camp on the Dalanta plateau till after dark, although the march commenced at five in the morning, and the rearguard and the baggage had for the most part to spend the night upon the road. Most of the Beloochees were thirty-six hours without food, but uttered no word of complaint. The Jidda was but a succession of stagnant pools, but even tyros in geology could distinguish marks which proved that in the rainy reason it must be a broad, deep, and rapid torrent.

On April 5, Sir Charles Staveley, with the 2nd Brigade, closed up to the Commander-in-Chief. For some days the force was delayed in the Dalanta plateau by want of supplies, which were ultimately obtained from the country in a considerable quantity, as the peasantry brought to the British lines grain which had been buried in order to conceal it from the marauders from Theodore's camp. On April 8, the head-quarters and one wing of the 45th Regiment arrived and joined the main body, which on the 9th moved forward five miles across the plain to the summit of the descent into the valley of the Bashilo, where it encamped within sight of the heights of Fahla, Selassie, Islamgi, and Magdála, around which the army of Theodore could be clearly distinguished. The descent to the river Bashilo, a distance of five miles, lay at the feet of the army, and in a plateau in the descent, the Punjab Pioneers and a wing of the Belooch battalion were stationed, to clear away any obstacles or make any improvements necessitated by the weather in Theodore's road.

On April 5, the Commander-in-Chief despatched by a native messenger, to King Theodore, a formal demand for the immediate and unconditional surrender of the prisoners, couched in these firm but moderate terms: 'By command of the Queen of England I am approaching Magdála with my army, in order to recover from your hands Envoy Rassam, Consul Cameron, Dr. Blanc, Lieutenant Prideaux, and the other Europeans now in your Majesty's power. I request your Majesty to send them to my camp as soon as it is sufficiently near to admit of their coming in safety.' This message was afterwards ascertained to have reached Theodore, but no answer was returned to it.

While the force was on the Dalanta plateau, scaling-ladders were prepared from the poles of the doolies, and sandbags were got ready. The weather was very much broken; rain and thunder were of nightly occurrence, and once or twice heavy hailstorms swept across the plain.

Sir Robert Napier now made arrangements to cut off Theodore's retreat from Magdála, in case he might attempt to fly and carry off with him the principal prisoners. Dejatch Mashesha was requested to occupy the Amba Kuheit, and cut off any retreat eastwards on the Bashilo. An envoy was sent to Masteeat, Queen of the Gallas, to induce her people to close any avenues from Magdála towards the south. This delicate mission was confided to Meer Akber Ali, a Mohammedan gentleman attached to the Intelligence Department, who gained the confidence of the Gallas through the profession of a similar creed.

Theodore had plundered these people, had taken away the women of their chiefs, handing over the young and comely to his soldiery, and retaining the older in prison: he had insulted them by reviling the name of their Prophet, and had forcibly converted to Christianity those whom he could seize. Each of the above deeds demands of a Moslem community that it should rise as one man to avenge it, and that life should be held for nought in the struggle. A war undertaken in such a cause is a Jahad, or sacred war, and is a religious obligation on all who profess to be followers of the Prophet. Any who lose life in such a struggle are considered martyrs; and if victory is impossible, it is incumbent on every Mohammedan to emigrate to some other country, and no longer endure such outrages.

The Gallas knew their obligations, but excused themselves for their supineness by pleading weakness; the vicinity of the British army, the exhortations of their priests, and the presence among them of an envoy from the British, whose faith had been outraged equally with their own, quickly induced them to determine to act against the common enemy. Arrangements were made by which a Galla chief, named Galla Eman, with two hundred men, should hold the road to Amba Geshen, so as to prevent Theodore's escape in that direction—having taken one of the most solemn Mohammedan oaths that they would not fail to do so. Having made this arrangement, Meer Akber Ali proceeded to the fort of Lugod, the residence of Masteeat, the Queen of the Gallas. Arrangements were made with Masteeat to hold the passes leading from Magdāla, which were afterwards found to be of some advantage.

These preparations were hardly completed, when Meer Akber Ali and the Gallas heard the sound of cannon, and news soon came in, to say that an engagement had taken place between the British and Theodore, in which the former had been completely victorious. At first the Gallas feared that the British would make peace with Theodore, and that, after the departure of his foreign foe, he would be able to wreak his vengeance on his Abyssinian enemies. A spy, however, came in from Magdāla, who reported that Theodore had sent messages to ask for peace from the British commander, who had refused to treat; that all the captives had been sent in safety to the British camp; that Theodore earnestly desired peace, and had sent a present of cattle to the British commander, who had declined to accept it. The Gallas were thus reassured, and armed the passes of Thaddat with musketeers and bushmen, who turned Theodore back on a later occasion, when he attempted to quit Magdála by the Kaffir-bir gate, which opens on the road towards Amba Geshen.

On the farther side of the Bashilo from that in which the British force was now encamped lay a rugged mass of broken ground, in the centre of which the Amba of Magdála rose to an almost equal height with the plateau of Dalanta. The rugged country, studded with a bushy vegetation, was bounded in the distance by the tablelands of Tanta and of Ambala Sieda. From the former the mountain mass of Magdála was separated by the ravine of the Menchura, from the latter by the Kulkulla torrent. Both of these were tributaries of the Bashilo. The mountain mass of Magdála forms a crescent, of which Magdála is the eastern horn, Fahla the western; midway between the two, in the centre, lies the plateau of Selassie, so called from a church upon it dedicated to the Trinity. Magdála and Selassie are connected by the saddle of Islamgi, and Selassie and Fahla by the saddle of Fahla. The highest of these plateaux is Magdála, which rises to a height of over 9,000 feet above the sea, and of 3,000 feet above the ravines of Menchara and Kulkulla. Its sides are scarped and steep, but at two points they fall upon the terraces of Islamgi and Sangallat. It is at these two points alone that an entrance can be made to the Amba by the Koket-bir and Kaffir-bir gates. From the foot of the Fahla saddle, the Wurki-Waha valley runs down to the Bashilo; up this ravine Theodore had constructed the road by which he had dragged his guns into position at Fahla. Between the upper portion of the stream which forms the valley and one of its tributaries lies the plain of Arogi. At the foot of the ascent to Fahla, and west of the same tributary at a higher elevation than the Arogi plain, lies the plateau of Afficho, which dips down towards the Bashilo in the rugged Gumbaji spur.

While the British army had been steadily approaching Magdāla, Theodore * had on March 1 commenced his descent into the valley of the Bashilo; on March 1 he crossed that river, on the 18th reached Arogi, and on the 25th pitched his camp upon Islamgi. On the mountains of Magdāla he then remained to await the attack of the British. As the advanced pioneers of the army of Sir Robert Napier moved down the slope leading to the Bashilo on April 9, Theodore watched them from Selassie, and looking through his telescope said, ' Hurrah ! there go the donkeys; we shall show them our prowess in battle.' The same day he issued fresh arms to his men, and after doing so began to drink arak. He spent the night in his tent in Islamgi, but before

---

* The text is fully corroborated by the statement made by Theodore's servant.

retiring to rest, he ordered three hundred and eighty prisoners belonging to all parts of the country to be brought down from Magdāla. These were brought down by the guard in the evening. He liberated Ras Engelda, chief of Agaomeder, Shum Saloron, of Tigre, and nearly one hundred others. Shortly afterwards the remainder raised a cry either for food or for freedom. The noise disturbed the King, who was intoxicated; he jumped up in a rage, and ordered them all to be put to death. He commenced the work of massacre himself, by cutting one of the bound women in two with his sword, and then drawing his pistol, shot two more. Three more were shot by one of his attendants, who was induced to do so by Theodore, and the remainder were hurled alive over the precipice—any who still showed signs of life were fired upon afterwards by the guards.

The King after this slept for three hours, and then spent much of the night in prayer. In his prayers he was heard to confess that he was drunk when he ordered the massacre, and to pray that it might not be laid to his charge. Before daybreak on the 10th he assembled his army, and ordered the road to be prepared for the passage of his guns from Magdāla to Fahla, where he posted four large guns and four smaller ones.

CHAPTER XI.

ACTION OF AROGI.

SIR ROBERT NAPIER, on April 7, had descended into the bed of the Bashilo, and reconnoitred the crossing of the river, which was a muddy stream about girth-deep. Magdāla lay twelve miles beyond the Bashilo; hence it was necessary, in order to make a closer reconnaissance of the fortress, to advance the force to a position whence staff-officers could, without inflicting serious toil upon their escorts, reconnoitre the approaches of Fahla and of the other outworks of the enemy's position. On April 10, at daybreak, the advance was commenced, and the whole of the army, with the exception of some cavalry, was moved down to the Bashilo. The ordinary approach to Magdāla from the Bashilo is by the Wurki-Waha ravine, up which Theodore had constructed his road: the road, on issuing from this ravine, scales the side of Fahla, a gigantic natural bastion level at the top, and is continually exposed to fire from the summits of Fahla and Selassie, and to the descent of rocks and stones. The Wurki-Waha valley is bounded on either side by high serrated spurs, which run down from Fahla and Selassie to the Bashilo. The enormous natural features of the country rendered it impossible for Sir Robert Napier, with his small force of infantry, to occupy both sides of the ravine. He recognised that Fahla was the key of Theodore's position, and determined to occupy the spur leading towards that important outwork which bears in different parts the names of Gumbaji and Afficho. When once established on this ridge, he could operate on either side of Fahla, as might seem expedient after a closer examination.

As the only supply of water between the Bashilo and Magdāla was under the enemy's fire, all the water-carriers of the force were organised, under command of Captain Bainbridge, for the purpose of carrying forward regular supplies of water from the river. The bandsmen and a party of the Punjab muleteers were also organised, under the command of Captain Griffith, and were furnished with stretchers for the removal of wounded men from the field.

On April 9 the following memorandum was issued from head-quarters:—

The 1st Brigade, 1st Division, with the exception of Cavalry under command of Brigadier-General Schneider, will take possession of the Gumbaji spur and encamp there to-morrow.

The Naval Brigade, A-21 R.A., and 74th Foot will march at daylight to-morrow morning to the bottom of the pass. One European Officer, 1 Native Officer, and 25 Sabres 3rd Cavalry will accompany this.

The four companies of the Sappers and Miners will accompany the 1st Brigade and make a road leading from the bed of the Bashilo on to the Gumbaji spur, under the direction of Captain Goodfellow, R.E.

The Infantry of the brigade now at the bottom of the pass will proceed to take possession of the spur in question when joined by Major-General Sir C. Staveley and Colonel Phayre.

The A-21 R.A. and Naval Brigade, with an escort of two companies of infantry, will remain on the bank of the Bashilo until the road is reported as practicable for laden mules by Captain Goodfellow, R.E.

Deputy-Quartermaster-General Colonel Phayre will accompany the 1st Brigade, and will make a reconnaissance towards Arogi and Fahla.

Brigadier-General Schneider will cover the reconnaissance with such a body of Infantry as he may consider necessary.

The 2nd Brigade will march to-morrow to the bed of the Bashilo at 10 A.M.

Captain Bainbridge will make arrangements for supplying the 1st Brigade with a proper supply of water.

The Head-quarters camp will be pitched with the 2nd Brigade.

By order,
(Signed) FRED. THESIGER, Colonel,
Dpy.-Adjt.-Genl., A.F.F.

Camp, Dalanta Plain,
April 9, 1868.

All preparations having been completed, the 3rd Bombay Light Cavalry, the 3rd Regiment of Sind Horse, and the 12th Bengal Cavalry were placed to hold the Bashilo, but were kept in readiness to advance, and the remainder of the force was moved across the river under the immediate command of Sir Charles Staveley. The 2nd Brigade, under Brigadier-General

Wilby, was ordered to remain in the bed of the Bashilo in support; while the infantry of the 1st Brigade, under Brigadier-General Schneider, was to occupy the Gumbaji spur, advance to a position suitable for an encampment, and at the same time cover a reconnaissance to be made by the Deputy-Quartermaster-General (Colonel Phayre) in the direction of Fahla. The guns, rocket battery, and baggage of the 1st Brigade were not to take the road up the Gumbaji spur, which was almost too severe for laden animals, until a road had been prepared by the Sappers and Miners, and had been reported practicable by Captain Goodfellow, the senior engineer officer. It is obvious that artillery and baggage could not have issued from the Wurki-Waha defile, unless the head of the defile was securely held, without exposing themselves to an attack from Fahla under every disadvantage. The 1st Brigade now consisted of :—

A Battery 21st Brigade Royal Artillery	86 men.
Royal Naval Brigade	80 ,,
10th Company Royal Engineers	20 ,,
1st Battalion 4th (King's Own) Regiment	446 ,,
23rd Punjab Pioneers	575 ,,
Wing 27th Beloochees	259 ,,
1st Company Madras Sappers	70 ,,
Bombay Sappers and Miners	283 ,,
	1819 ,,

A small detachment of the 3rd Bombay Light Cavalry marched with the 1st Brigade as a support.

Colonel Phayre, supported by Brigadier-General

Schneider, started on his reconnaissance. The troops toiled painfully and slowly up the rugged slopes of the Gumbaji spur: they suffered severely from the difficult nature of the path, great heat, and want of water, and many fell out of the ranks exhausted by fatigue.

The four companies of Sappers were to make with the utmost expedition a path up the Gumbaji spur for the guns, rocket battery and baggage of the 1st Brigade.

Colonel Phayre having no other Infantry at hand, unfortunately took the Sappers as his escort, and the road remained unmade.

The Commander-in-Chief, when commencing the ascent to Gumbaji, received a report from Colonel Phayre, forwarded through Sir C. Staveley, saying that having got the head of the pass the Sappers would be left to secure it, and the guns and baggage might take that route.

On receiving this report Sir Robert Napier ordered the guns of the A Battery, the Naval Rocket Brigade and the baggage of the 1st Brigade to move up by the King's road, the issue of which he believed that Colonel Phayre had secured.

He then proceeded towards the front, and on his way passed the weary and exhausted soldiers of the Infantry Brigade, including the Sappers and Miners. Sir Robert arrived on the Afficho plateau at the same time as the head of the column which was formed by Chamberlain's Pioneers.

He then perceived, much to his astonishment after the tenor of Colonel Phayre's report, that at the point where the King's road emerged from the Wurki-Waha ravine, at a distance of 1,200 yards from him, and 700 feet below him, there were no troops stationed, and none nearer to it than Chamberlain's Pioneers on the Afficho plateau. Immediately, to repair the obvious error, he ordered Sir C. Staveley to move quickly Chamberlain's Pioneers to the left, and secure the head of the pass, and sent back speedy messengers to hurry up the whole brigade. He was none too soon, for the leading mules of Penn's batteries were already emerging from the pass. A few moments after they came in view, a puff of white smoke curled up from the summit of Fahla, a roundshot whirred over the heads of the staff and buried itself heavily in the ground behind, the report of a heavy piece of ordnance woke the echoes of the basaltic cliffs of Magdála, and, as if by a preconcerted signal, the steep path and the mountain-sides of Fahla were instantaneously covered by masses of warriors, quickly rushing down to seize, as they hoped, wealthy booty from an unsuspecting foe.

For Theodore had watched the appearance of the laden mules, and, imagining that they only bore baggage, had told his soldiery to go down and seize them—not, however, without some hesitation. They were led by his favourite general, and rushed down to battle as men accustomed to victory. He himself remained on Fahla, to direct the fire of his artillery, which maintained a perpetual cannonade against the heads of the British columns; but, from too elevated a position, its fire was plunging, and from the use of too heavy charges of powder it ranged too far, so that it caused no casualties. Among the assailant Abyssinians, who numbered not less than 5,000, there were no regular cavalry, but the principal chiefs, about 500 in number, were mounted, and gorgeously attired in scarlet.

The Naval Brigade hastened up the road to the Afficho plateau, and as each rocket-tube came into position, it opened on the advancing masses of the enemy, who were startled, and slightly checked; but one portion advanced, nevertheless, with great confidence against the position of the head of the British column on the plateau, while another bore down towards the head of the pass to attack the artillery and baggage.

Sir Robert Napier ordered Sir Charles Staveley to prepare the troops to receive the enemy; the latter directed Brigadier-General Schneider to cause them to lay down their packs and to advance. The 4th (King's Own) Regiment, in skirmishing order, under Colonel Cameron, closely followed, and, supported by the wing of the Beloochees under Major Beville, the detachment of Royal Engineers under Major Pritchard, and the

Bombay Sappers under Captain MacDonnell, descended rapidly the steep path which led down from the Afficho Plateau into the dip of the ground which separated it from the Arogi plain. The troops cheered loudly as they saw at last the chance of a close contest with the enemy whom they had so long been approaching. As the men of the 4th Regiment emerged from this dip, and rose upon the brow of the Arogi plain, extending as they pushed forward, they came close upon the advancing masses of Abyssinians. They opened fire immediately, and the bullets, shot in rapid succession from their breechloading arms, told with fearful effect upon their assailants. The latter were driven back, but slowly and stubbornly; they fired constantly, and made several attempts to rally and charge; but the line of skirmishers bore steadily forward, and the main portion of the Abyssinians, after the loss of many chiefs, were driven off the plain of Arogi, down the slopes which led into the ravines at the head of the Wurki-Waha defile. A portion retired up the side of the Fahla hill, and, taking cover in a thick grove of cactus-trees, opened a teasing fire on Staveley's right, which caused him some loss.

Another party of the enemy attempted to pass round the sides of the Afficho Plateau, and to turn Staveley's right; but were checked by the discharge of a few rockets, and by the exertions of the K Company of Madras Sappers, under Major Prendergast, supported by Lieutenant-Colonel Loch with his detachment of Bombay Cavalry. Captain Fellowes, of the Naval Brigade, maintained the fire of his rockets until it was masked by the advance of the infantry. He was then moved forward to join Sir Charles Staveley; and the fire of the rockets, together with some volleys from the Beloochees and Engineers, supported by two of Penn's guns, which were brought up to the right flank under Lieutenant Taylor, cleared Staveley's flank from all further annoyance. The fire of the rockets was then directed upon the summit of Fahla; they were well aimed, and, as was subsequently ascertained, one very nearly killed Theodore, who was there engaged in directing the operations of his artillery, now reduced at that point to six guns, as his monster piece of ordnance, 'Theodorus,' burst at its first discharge.

In the meantime a sharp action had been fought at the point where the King's Road issued from the Wurki-Waha valley. Colonel Milward had ascended from that defile with Penn's battery, escorted by detachments of the 4th (King's Own) Regiment, and of the 23rd Pioneers. On seeing the troops of Theodore rushing down the mountain-side, Colonel Milward hastily threw his force into position beside the Punjab Pioneers, and opened fire with Penn's battery. A large body of Abyssinians bore down upon the position occupied by Milward's guns and Chamberlain's Pioneers. Notwithstanding the effects of the mountain artillery, they continued to advance with much determination and order. Chamberlain, with his Pioneers, advanced promptly to meet them; both sides rushed in fearlessly, and a close contest ensued between spears and bayonets; for the men of the Punjab did not possess breechloading arms, and could not load so rapidly as the European soldiers. Not without a gallant resistance, in which many spear-wounds were received, were the Abyssinians forced off, and urged with great slaughter into the ravines on Chamberlain's left front.

Farther on the left, considerable numbers of the enemy pressed towards the head of the defile, where the baggage had arrived. With great readiness the baggage-master, Lieutenant Sweny, of the King's Own Regiment, massed the baggage in a safe position; and the baggage-guard, consisting of two companies of the King's Own Regiment and one of the 10th Native Infantry, were brought forward, and effectually checked the attempt of the enemy to penetrate into the defile. Arrested at the head of the ravine by the baggage-guard, closed in upon by Chamberlain's Pioneers and two companies of the 4th Regiment, which Sir Charles Staveley wheeled up against their flank, this portion of the enemy suffered most severely. Large numbers fell, from the fire of the guns and the rapid discharges of the Snider rifles.

It was four o'clock in the afternoon when the first

gun, which announced the opening of the engagement, was fired from Fahla; it was seven o'clock, and nearly dark, before the Abyssinian soldiery were completely driven off. A thunderstorm and heavy rain had continued during the greater part of the action. When finally repelled, the troops of Theodore spread in no hasty or disorganised flight; they returned again and again to the attack, wherever the ground favoured them. They had advanced with the full confidence of men accustomed to victory, and had cast away all the advantages of their defensive position to close more rapidly with their enemy. They had been promised by Theodore that they should be enriched by the spoils of the English, and it was not without a stout resistance that the last of them were finally driven off the field. Orders were then issued, by Sir Robert Napier, to prevent the pursuit being carried too far up the hill, as such a manœuvre could only have terminated by the British being obliged to retire, which might have given renewed confidence to the now prostrated army of Theodore.

The British troops, thoroughly wet and tired, but highly elated with their victory, bivouacked for the night on the ground which covered the issue of the Wurki-Waha valley, in order to protect the baggage, which was still in the ravine. During the night the 2nd Brigade marched up the valley from the Bashilo, and before daylight occupied this position; while the

1st Brigade, on being relieved, reoccupied the commanding position on Afficho, from which it had descended to encounter the enemy.

The wounded were promptly attended to after the action, and many wounded Abyssinians were also carried off the field by the British troops, and carefully tended in the British hospitals. The probable number of Abyssinians lost was computed at 700 killed and 1,200 wounded, including many chiefs of note—among whom was the Fitaurari Gabri, to whom Theodore had entrusted the conduct of the army in the battle, and who was considered as the right-hand of the King himself. Nearly all night the calls of the Abyssinians to their wounded friends were heard, and the greater number of the latter were carried off the field. Lights could also be seen burning up and down the steep ascent of Fahla, which at first were supposed to betoken a night-attack by Theodore on the British lines, but were only borne by the friends and relatives of those who came to seek some one either killed or wounded on the Arogi plain.

The British loss amounted only to twenty wounded, two of which were mortal cases. The great disparity of loss was due to the determined and persistent attack of the Abyssinians against the better-disciplined and better-armed force of the British, and to the invincible courage with which the Punjab Pioneers, whose smoothbore musket was hardly equal to the double-barrelled percussion-gun of the Abyssinians, repaired the deficiencies of that weapon by a stern use of the bayonet.

Theodore had watched the fight from Fahla, where he superintended his artillery, which was fired by Abyssinians; but Mr. Saalmüller, Waldmeier, and the other artisans, were required to weigh out the charge for each gun. When the British opened upon Fahla, the rockets ranged to the place where Theodore was standing, and one killed a horse close behind him. He exclaimed, 'What a terrible weapon!—who can fight against it?' Then he covered himself with his shield, and watched the battle in silence. At one time those around the King saw the British skirmishers take ground to the rear; they raised a shout of triumph, and sent off news of victory to Magdála. But as night came on the King sent a messenger to Fitaurari Gabri, to ask what was the news. The messenger returned to say that that chief could not be found. He was sent back for more accurate intelligence, and afterwards returned with the report that Gabri was killed. Theodore named one after the other of his chiefs, and the answer was always that they were dead. The men who had escaped from the battle had gone to their homes in Islamgi. Theodore saw that his army was broken and destroyed. On Selassie, sleepless, in bitter thought, he passed the night, the stillness of which was perpetually broken by loud peals of angry thunder, and the shrill though distant cries of those who sought for the wounded, or mourned the dead, down below at Arogi.

Next morning the valley of Arogi showed all the naked horrors of a battlefield. 'Tracks of blood marked the courses of the wounded, who had spent their last efforts in feeble attempts to crawl back to the fortress and live, or to gain the shelter of some neighbouring bush to die. The body of Fitaurari Gabri could be distinguished from the remainder of the fallen by its gorgeous attire. The splendid shirt, which had been the oriflamme of the Abyssinian forces the previous evening, and which had made the wearer supposed to be Theodore himself, and to be the mark of many a bullet, could be recognised by all. He had been one of the first to fall; and seven chiefs, who had attempted to bear away his body, were laid in a heap around him.

' On the left, where the Pioneers and baggage-guard had been engaged, the dead lay thickest. Along the ravine where the bayonet-charge was made, men and horses were heaped in tens and twenties. In some cases the sword and bayonet had completed what the bullet had left but half-done; all that lay there had been dead a long time before morning. On the right, where the firing had been at longer ranges, the tale of dead was not so great, and more wounded men lay around, awaiting without a murmur or repine the approaching termination of their sufferings. The claims of these to sympathy were not disregarded. Many a dying man was turned to ease his pain, and many a flask was emptied of its precious contents, at the dumb request of some fevered lip or parched tongue. In addition to those that lay there, hundreds had been carried into the fortress during the night. The rockets and shells left abundant testimony that the consternation and dismay which they had caused among the Abyssinians were far from groundless. Many a charred mass and mangled heap showed how terrible was the havoc, how awful the death they carried wherever they sped. Before a week elapsed, the sleek wolves and greedy vultures deprived the field of much of its horror, giving it the appearance, which it long will retain, of a place of skulls.' *

* Shepherd's Abyssinian Campaign.

CHAPTER XII.

SURRENDER OF THE CAPTIVES.

ABOUT midnight, Theodore, after brooding over the disasters of the day, sent Mr. Flad and Mr. Waldmeier to Mr. Rassam's house at Magdála with the following message : ' I thought that the people that are now coming were women—I now find that they are men. I have been conquered by the advance-guard alone. All my gunners are dead : reconcile me with your people.'

Returning to the King's tent, Messrs. Flad and Waldmeier informed him of their arrival by one of the eunuchs, who had accompanied them for that purpose. In the meantime Theodore had been drinking hard : he came out of his tent very excited, and asked the Europeans, 'What do you want?' They told him that, as he had commanded them, they had spoken on his behalf to Mr. Rassam, who had proposed to send Lieutenant Prideaux as an envoy into the British camp. Theodore interrupted them, and in an angry voice exclaimed, 'Mind your own business—go to your tents!' The two Europeans stood still, in the hope that he might change his mind; but, seeing that they did not depart, he became angry, and in a high tone of voice ordered them to retire at once.

At about four o'clock in the morning, a messenger was sent by Theodore to call Messrs. Flad and Waldmeier before him. As soon as they arrived he said, 'Do you hear this wailing? There is not a soldier who has not lost a friend or a brother! What will it be when the whole army comes? What shall I do? Counsel me.' Mr. Waldmeier told him, 'Your Majesty, peace is best.' 'And you, Flad, what do you say?' 'Your Majesty,' replied Mr. Flad, 'ought to accept Mr. Rassam's proposal.' The King remained a few minutes silent, apparently in deep thought, and then said, 'Well, go back to Magdála, and tell Mr. Rassam that I trust in his friendship to reconcile me with his people. I will do what he thinks best.'

At daybreak, accordingly, Lieutenant Prideaux, with Mr. Flad and Dejatch Alami, a son-in-law and confidential chief of Theodore, started for the British lines.* By dawn the two British brigades had taken up their positions on the Afficho Plateau and the Arogi plain. The Beloochees were being pushed forward slowly in skirmishing order, so as to cover the force, when a small body of horsemen could be descried slowly winding down the road from Magdála towards the camp. A white flag of truce could be made out, and the uniform of a British officer among them. The

* Dr. Blanc.

news burst through the ranks like wildfire, and, amidst loud cheers and rapturous greetings, Lieutenant Prideaux passed through the outposts, and was escorted by a jubilant crowd to the tent of the Commander-in-Chief.

Lieutenant Prideaux and Mr. Flad delivered a verbal message from Theodore, to the effect that till yesterday he had thought himself the greatest man in the world, but that he had now found out that there were others stronger than he, and he desired to be reconciled to the British Government. But reconciliation on any terms short of submission it was not in the power of Sir Robert Napier to afford to Theodore. The Commander-in-Chief was required to remove Theodore from Abyssinia, and, confident in his intention of fulfilling his instructions, he had received aid and supplies from the various peoples of Abyssinia, who would have suffered wofully after the departure of the British if Theodore had been allowed to retain his mountain stronghold, or any vestige of his formidable power. The only answer which Sir Robert Napier could return to the verbal message of the King was written in the following letter :—

Your Majesty has fought like a brave man, and has been overcome by the superior power of the British army.

It is my desire that no more blood may be shed. If, therefore, your Majesty will submit to the Queen of England, and bring all the Europeans now in your Majesty's hands, and deliver them safely this day in the British camp, I guarantee honourable treatment for yourself and for all the members of your Majesty's family.

In the meantime Dejatch Alami was shown the mortars and the elephants before his return, and was told that the arms used in the action of the previous evening, in which Dejatch Alami had been present, were but mere playthings in comparison to these destroying machines; and he was assured by Sir Robert Napier, that if the King did not surrender and give up the captives, the big mortars and the Armstrong guns would be sent up against him, and that then none of his soldiers would escape alive. On taking leave to return, Dejatch Alami said to Mr. Flad: 'There is no escape for us (meaning the King and his followers); we must surrender, or we shall be killed. We have no chance to run away; they would pursue us, and we are surrounded by our enemies, the plundered Warro Haimanoo people and the Wollo Gallas. I am almost sure that the King will send down the captives, but I fear he won't go down himself, partly from fear, and partly from being mortified.'

It must have been trying for Lieutenant Prideaux and Mr. Flad, after having once set their feet within the British lines, to be forced to return to the presence and into the power of such a capricious and cruel despot as Theodore. Equally was it trying to Sir Robert Napier, on whose slightest action or word hung the lives of so many prisoners, still within Theodore's power, to insist upon terms which it must have been evident the still proud though defeated monarch by no means contemplated.

The envoys, who were instructed to say that the body of Fitaurari Gabri might be removed to Magdāla, returned up the hill, and found Theodore on Selassie. The letter of Sir Robert Napier was twice translated by Mr. Flad and Mr. Waldmeier to the King, and by the questions that he put it was evident that he fully understood what Sir Robert Napier required of him.* He asked, 'What do they mean by honourable treatment? Do they mean to treat me honourably as their prisoner, or do they intend to assist me in recovering my country from the rebels? And have they taken into account my numerous family, for I have as many wives and children almost as I have hairs on my head? It would involve immense expense in England if they would undertake to provide for them all.' To this Prideaux replied, that the Commander-in-Chief did not give any further information than what was in the letter. Mr. Waldmeier suggested that the King ought to write again to request further information on these points.

Theodore then ordered the envoys to go aside and take a seat, while he dictated a paper to his secretary. The tone of this letter was probably influenced by the fact that during the short interval, while the letter was

---

* Mr. Flad's statement.

being written, the whole of the soldiers of the King, armed and arrayed for battle, came and took up a position in Selassie; and that, as the loss sustained in the previous action was found not to be so great as at first anticipated, Theodore contemplated an attack on the British camp, especially as the soldiers were heard to say, 'The English are fond of sleeping; we must attack them in the middle of the night, and we will utterly destroy them ere they will get awake.' The document contained in the same cover Sir Robert Napier's letter of the morning, which Theodore returned, as he considered himself insulted, because the servant of a woman had presumed to address him at all. It was not in the form of a letter, as he considered it beneath his dignity to hold any correspondence with Sir Robert Napier; neither was it sealed. The translation of its contents was as follows:—

In the name of the Father, and the Son, and the Holy Ghost, one God in His Trinity and His Unity:

Kâsa, whose trust is in Christ, thus speaks:

O people of Abyssinia! will it always be thus that you flee before the enemy, when I myself, by the power of God, go not forth with you to encourage you?

Believing that all power had been given to me, I had established my Christian people in this heathen spot. In my city are multitudes whom I had fed—maids protected and maidens unprotected; women whom yesterday made widows, and aged parents who have no children. God has given you the power. See that you forsake not these people. It is a heathen land.

My countrymen have turned their backs on me and have hated me, because I imposed tribute on them, and sought to bring them under military discipline. You have prevailed against me by means of people brought into a state of discipline.

My followers, who loved me, were frightened by one bullet, and fled in spite of my command. When you defeated them I was not with the fugitives.

Believing myself to be a great lord, I gave you battle; but, by reason of the worthlessness of my artillery, all my pains were as nought.

The people of my country, by taunting me with having embraced the religion of the Franks, and by saying that I had become a Mussulman, and in ten different ways, had provoked me to anger against them. Out of what I have done of evil towards them may God bring good! His will be done! I had intended, if God had so decreed, to conquer the whole world, and it was my desire to die if my purpose could not be fulfilled. Since the day of my birth till now no man has dared to lay hands on me. Whenever my soldiers began to waver in battle, it was mine to arise and rally them. Last night the darkness hindered me from doing so.

You people, who have passed the night in joy, may God do unto you as He has done to me! I had hoped, after subduing all my enemies in Abyssinia, to lead my army against Jerusalem, and expel from it the Turks. A warrior who has dandled strong men in his arms like infants will never suffer himself to be dandled in the arms of others.

It was an anxious hour for Sir Robert Napier when he received his returned letter from the hands of Prideaux and Flad. It was hard to leave countrymen to what seemed certain massacre, but he considered that a fuller atonement than the surrender of the captives, when they could no longer be retained, was absolutely required, and must be exacted; and, painful as was the thought of the possible consequences to the captives if Theodore's rage should become excited, Sir Robert Napier relied for their safety on the apprehension of a renewal of the conflict which demoralised Theodore's troops—an apprehension from which Theodore himself was not entirely free, as was involuntarily betrayed by Dejatch Alami. Sir Robert Napier also relied on his threat, which he had impressed on Dejatch Alami, of unrelenting pursuit and of punishment of all who might in any way be concerned in the ill-treatment of the European captives; and he had pointed out how the power of Great Britain had already reached Magdāla, and that no corner of Abyssinia, however remote, could screen anyone whom England was determined to punish. It was a sad parting when Prideaux and Flad set out on their return to the mountain, bearers of the same letter which Sir Robert Napier had entrusted to them in the morning, and instructed to intimate that the British Commander would grant no other terms than those contained therein; for they themselves, and all others, considered that they ran the risk of any hasty resolve or any sudden fury of drunkenness on the part of the semi-barbarous King.

But this sorrow was destined to be turned into joy. After the despatch of his insulting missive, Theodore had spent some time in meditation and prayer. He called a council of his advisers, when Ras Engedda, the prime minister, Dejatch Abaye, Dejatch Wahe, and others, strongly recommended the murder of the captives, and resistance to the last; but Basha Avito (who had been in the British camp) and Dejatch Alami urged that the English had come all this way for their countrymen, who were of no use to Abyssinia, while, if they were killed, terrible vengeance would be taken. To these the King listened with favour, and sent Ras Assani to Magdála, to release the captives and bring them to him. While the messenger was absent, the King, suddenly enraged at the idea of surrender, drew his double-barrelled pistol, and placed it in his mouth. Ras Engeda rushed forward, to seize him and prevent the act of suicide. The pistol was wrested from his mouth, but in the struggle was discharged, and the bullet grazed his ear. Theodore then covered his head with a cloth, lay down upon the ground, gradually becoming composed, and was only aroused by the intelligence that Mr. Rassam was approaching. He had an interview with Mr. Rassam, and it will probably be never accurately known what passed at that final meeting. It is certain that Theodore believed that Mr. Rassam was a man of immense influence in England, and that his counsels in the British camp would be heard with every respect—a point upon which it is not probable that Mr. Rassam would undeceive him. It is also certain that Mr. Rassam promised Theodore that he would return, to report to him what amelioration of the terms of peace could be obtained from the British commander, a promise which Mr. Rassam afterwards avowed he had no intention of observing; and it is not impossible that Mr. Rassam may, besides a promise which he would not perform, have made others of a favourable peace, which he could not perform, when anxious to secure the temporary goodwill of the excitable monarch. The result was that Mr. Rassam, the remainder of the British captives, and several of those of other nations, were dismissed to the British camp, and Mr. Mayer was sent in advance to announce their approach. He, as he descended the hill, met Mr. Flad and Lieutenant Prideaux returning. These also now turned back, and one hour after sunset Mr. Rassam arrived in the camp a free man, and with him came Consul Cameron, Dr. Blanc, Mr. Stern, Mr. and Mrs. Rosenthal, Mr. Kerans, and Pietro. These had all been liberated. They were escorted, on the part of the King, by the artisans Mr. Mayer, Mr. Waldmeier, Mr. Saalmüller, and Mr. Moritz, and by Dejatch Alami and Aito Samuel. It was not understood whether the German artisans had been liberated by the King, or were expected to return to him. It was judged by Sir Robert Napier better that they should return to Magdála the next morning, until regularly discharged by Theodore.

Although matters had thus assumed a most hopeful aspect, yet there remained ground for anxiety. Mrs. Flad, whose Christian fortitude during all her trials gained for her universal esteem, was still in the hands of Theodore, as she was unable, on account of weak health, to undertake the journey down the mountain that night, as were also the families of the German artisans and other Europeans, for whom Sir Robert Napier was bound to take thought. It was believed that they too had been liberated, and had only been prevented by illness, or other causes not resting with the King, from leaving the *amba*. Still the uncertain and dangerous temper of Theodore was too well known to prevent the life of anyone being considered perfectly safe while still within his reach.

That same Saturday afternoon as Theodore dismissed the British captives, he seems to have turned some thought to the wrongs which he had inflicted on his rightful Queen, Tirrowark. She had for long years been placed in Magdāla with her little boy Alumayou,[*] while Theodore had been leading an irregular life at Debra Tabor, and had lately insulted his Queen by the presence in Magdāla of his favourite concubine—a fat, voluptuous Yedjow Galla woman, named Itamangu, who, while the Queen was neglected, received an almost daily letter from the King. On the afternoon of the 11th he sent a request to Tirrowark to visit him

[*] 'I have seen the world.'

at his tent in Islamgi, and they passed there some time together.

Early on the following morning (that of Easter Sunday) Sir Robert Napier received, by the hands of the King's scribe, Alaka Ingada, and Mr. Bender, one of his German artisans, an Amharic letter, which was translated verbally by Aito Samuel from Amharic into Arabic, and by Mr. Rassam from Arabic into English. In this letter Theodore endeavoured to apologise for the tone which he had adopted in his communication of the previous day, and explained that he had written the former document after he had made up his mind to take away his life. He related how his attempt to carry out his design had failed, and that he now desired friendship, and was prepared to send down at once every European, along with an offering of a few cows, as it was the Easter festival. The letter was duly signed and sealed with the royal seal, and ran as follows:—

In the name of the Father, the Son, and the Holy Ghost, one God:

The King of Kings Theôderos:

May it reach the beloved servant of the Great Queen of England.

I am writing to you, without being able to address you by name, because our intercourse has arisen so unexpectedly.

I am grieved at having sent you my writing of yesterday, and at having quarrelled with you, my friend. When I saw your manner of fighting, and the discipline of your army, and when my people failed to execute my orders, then I was consumed with sorrow to think that, although I killed and punished my soldiers, yet they would not return to the battle. Whilst the fire of jealousy burned within me, Satan came to me in the night, and tempted me to kill myself with my own pistol. But, reflecting that God would be angry with me if I were to go in this manner, and leave my army without a protector, I sent to you in a hurry lest I might die, and all things be in confusion before my message should reach you. After my messenger had gone, I cocked my pistol, and, putting it in my mouth, pulled the trigger. Though I pulled and pulled, yet it would not go off. But when my people rushed upon me, and laid hold of the pistol, it was discharged, just as they had drawn it from my mouth. God having thus signified to me that I should not die but live, I sent to you Mr. Rassam that same evening, that your heart might be made easy.

To-day is Easter; be pleased to let me send a few cows to you.

The reason of my returning to you your letter yesterday, was that I believed at that time that we should meet one another in heaven, but never on earth.

I let the night pass without sending for the body of my friend Fitaurari Gabri, because I thought that after my death we should both be buried together; but since I have lived, be pleased to allow him to be buried.

You require from me all the Europeans, even to my best friend Waldmeier. Well, be it so; they shall go. But, now that we are friends, you must not leave me without artisans, as I am a lover of the mechanical arts.

This letter was translated by Aito Samuel from Amharic into Arabic, and by Mr. Rassam from Arabic into English, in the presence of Colonel Merewether, Mr. Flad, and Lieutenant Tweedie. Colonel Merewether pointed out that the letter contained nothing which should tend to cause an alteration in the arrangements already made for the return of Mr. Flad and the German artisans to the mountain, to bring down Mrs. Flad and the wives and children of the others. The Commander-in-Chief sent a verbal answer, which was to be taken to Theodore by Samuel and Dejatch Alami, which said that 'a palanquin was sent up for Mrs. Flad because she was not well, and that Sir Robert Napier desired the King to send her and all the other Europeans that same day down to the British camp.' This allowed no semblance of any amelioration of the terms offered to the King on the previous day.

Mr. Rassam, in his confidential Report, states regarding Theodore's letter, that 'Alaka Ingada read it; Samuel translated it to me in Arabic while I rendered it word by word to Sir R. Napier in English. As Samuel was ordered by the King to take the answer, and was required to go up and assist in bringing to the British camp the European artisans and their families, he asked what reply he was to take to the King with regard to a present of cows and sheep which was offered by the King in his letter.'

'On communicating this question to the Commander-in-Chief, His Excellency said, "I accept them."'

Colonel Merewether distinctly denies the correctness of this statement, and gives the following account:—
'On the conclusion of the translation of Theodore's

letter, Colonel Merewether pointed out that as there was nothing in the letter affecting the previous arrangement for the departure of Mr. Flad and the others, they had better depart, and a reply could follow. Orders were given accordingly.

' In two or three minutes Mr. Rassam returned with Samuel, and asked the Commander-in-Chief what answer was to be given about the cattle; were they accepted?

' The Commander-in-Chief, without apparently giving any particular thought, or attempting to discuss the question in any way, simply bowed his head, but did not utter a word.

'Evidently the Commander-in-Chief considered the matter of small importance, not affecting the main point, namely, the terms which had been offered the King, and which had more than once been communicated to him—unconditional surrender, when honourable treatment would be accorded to him and his family.' *

As Mr. Rassam was the vehicle of communication between Samuel and the Commander-in-Chief, and was the only one present who could translate from English into Arabic, it is evident that Samuel could only have acquired his views of the acceptance or non-acceptance of the cattle from Mr. Rassam. Mr. Flad has shown, in his statement, that as he returned to the mountain

* Statements of Colonel Merewether and Lieutenant Tweedie.

with Samuel, the latter was of opinion that the cattle had not been accepted, at least certainly not as a peace-offering, because Mr. Flad said to Samuel on the way, 'What about the cattle?' Samuel replied, 'They are accepted.' 'Then,' said Mr. Flad, 'it will be peace;' to which Samuel replied, 'What does it matter to you whether it will be peace or not? Make haste and get away with your wife from the mountain. Would it not be well if Theodore, who has oppressed us all, should be removed from Abyssinia?'* Such was the view which Mr. Rassam's confidant held of the affair of the cattle. In the course of the afternoon, Colonel Thesiger learnt that a large number of cattle were being sent down from Theodore as a peace-offering. He immediately reported this new phase of the case to the Commander-in-Chief, who, on hearing the magnitude and nature of the offering, was surprised and indignant, and sent immediate orders to the outlying picquets that the cattle should not be admitted.

The offered tribute of cattle appears to have been a deliberate ruse devised by Theodore, or suggested to him, for the purpose of precluding Sir Robert Napier from further hostile action. If the British Commander had accepted a large present from Theodore one day, and had attacked him the next, it would have been a violation of the commonly accepted *jus gentium* of Abyssinia, especially if the circumstance were looked

* Statement of Mr. Flad.

at by itself, and without reference to the fact that Theodore had on the previous day been plainly told that nothing but his own surrender of himself would satisfy the British Government. It is remarkable that Mr. Rassam, who was so well acquainted with the Abyssinian mind, and who acted as Sir Robert Napier's interpreter on the occasion, did not warn the Commander-in-Chief against the snare laid for him in the matter of the cattle, especially as Mr. Rassam had spent the previous night in the company of the released captives, and was fully aware of the demand of unconditional surrender on the part of the King on which Sir Robert Napier was determined to insist. Whether this remissness on the part of Mr. Rassam was due to any still unknown occurrences which took place at his interview with Theodore on the previous day, while Mr. Rassam was still in the King's power, it is impossible certainly to say.

The four Germans who had escorted Mr. Rassam's party down the evening before, with Dejatch Alami, Mr. Flad, and Samuel, returned to the mountain. It was not considered necessary to send back Lieutenant Prideaux, as he belonged to Mr. Rassam's party, which had been formally dismissed. They took up with them the remains of the Abyssinian leader of Friday, the Fituarari Gabri. The King, as well as other Abyssinians, was pleased with this act of generosity on the part of the English General. The body was immediately interred at Magdála. On reaching the King's camp, the messengers found him seated outside of his tent. Dejatch Alami delivered the compliments of Sir Robert Napier to the King, with an acknowledgment of the arrival in the British camp of Mr. Rassam's party, and a reiterated demand that the remainder of the Europeans should be sent down. Theodore at once replied, 'Well, I give every one of them permission to leave Magdála.' The King then asked whether, at the time when Mr. Flad and his companions had left the British camp, the letter carried by his scribe and Mr. Bender had arrived. Aito Samuel replied, 'that the letter was presented to the Commander-in-Chief, and translated.' The King enquired what answer had been given about the offered cattle. Samuel told him that Sir Robert Napier had expressed his willingness to accept them. The King then ordered 1,000 cattle and 500 sheep to be sent down to the British camp, and told Mr. Flad to take his wife and children, and go down with Dejatch Alami and the cattle; but as Mrs. Flad was unable to be hurried down so quickly, on account of her illness, Mr. Waldmeier was ordered to go down with the cattle. Yet Theodore did not seem confident of the reception of the cattle. He withdrew his artillery from Fahla, but posted it in a prepared position in the market-place of Islamgi, to cover the approach to Magdála. When he heard that the cattle were stopped at the picquets, the artisans,

SURRENDER OF THE CAPTIVES.

their women and baggage, had not yet left the mountain. Theodore sent for them; and when they came, he ordered them to go down to the British camp, and on seeing them depart, said to his chiefs, 'Surely it is peace, now they have taken my power from me—surely it is peace!' But even after the arrival of the artisans, the cattle were still held without the British sentries. Theodore saw that he could not obtain peace without his personal surrender. He went into the *amba*, and spent a restless night.*

That afternoon all the Europeans who had been held in captivity by the Abyssinian King arrived in camp, except the Frenchman M. Bardel, who was struck down with fever and sunstroke, and who, when of no further use to Theodore, had been sent out of Magdála, and located in a miserable hovel in Islamgi. The following is the list of the restored captives:—

Mr. Rassam; Consul Cameron; Mr. Flad, Mrs. Flad, and three children; Lieutenant Prideaux, Bombay Army; Dr. Blanc, Bombay Army; Rev. Mr. Stern; Mr. Rosenthal, Mrs. Rosenthal, and one child; Mr. Kerans; Pietro, servant of Consul Cameron (Italian); Mr. Staiger, German missionary, sent by a Scotch Society; Mr. Brandies, as above; Mr. Essler, German and naturalist; Mr. Schiller, ditto; M. Makerer, Frenchman, a servant, originally of Consul Cameron, latterly of Theodore; M. Zander (German), King's artisan, native wife, and four children; Mr. Waldmeier (Swiss), as above, an Abyssinian wife (who is the late Mr. Bell's daughter), and one child; Mr. Saalmüller (German),

---

* Accounts of Mr. Flad and Theodore's gun-bearer.

as above, wife (viz., daughter of Bell), and one child; Aleegas (son of late Mr. Bell), an artisan ; Mr. Bender (German), wife and three children; Mrs. Kenzlen, widow of a German artisan, and one child; Mr. Moritz, wife and child; Mr. Mayer (German), artisan, wife and three childron ; M. Bourgaud (French), artisan, French wife and five children ; Mr. Schimper (German), geographer, &c. ; Mr. Schimper, jun., an artisan; Mr. M'Kelvie (Irishman), servant of Consul Cameron ; Mr. John Parkins, artisan ; M. Bardel (Frenchman).

CHAPTER XIII.

CAPTURE OF MAGDĀLA.

AT sunrise on the morning of Easter Monday, April 13, Theodore arose, and, calling to his troops, said: 'Warriors who love me, gird yourselves; leave all behind, take nothing but arms, and follow me; the time has come to seek another home.' He had apparently determined to make an attempt to escape, and went out of the fortress near the Kaffir-bir Gate, at a place where it was possible to descend towards Sangallat.* He was followed by two chiefs of rank, and about two thousand men, variously armed. As he passed down, he asked where the advance-guard was, and on being told that they were in rear, ordered them to the front. They refused, saying that they would never flee before an enemy again, and would rather seek death in Magdāla. Theodore pondered for a brief space, and then, saying, 'Let it be so,' reascended the mountain. It would have been impossible for him to continue his journey alone, as the cries of the Gallas— who, under the guidance of Meer Akber Ali, were

---

* Statement of Waldo Gabir, gun-bearer to Theodore, who was with him.

watching the issue from the fortress on that side—could be distinctly heard. On re-entering the fortress, he told all who were not prepared to share his fortunes to the last to provide for their own safety. Thousands thereupon left him, and ultimately surrendered to the British.

Sir Robert Napier, at the request of Dejatch Alami, had promised to abstain from hostilities for twenty-four hours. By Monday morning forty-eight hours had elapsed, but the prescribed conditions had not been complied with, and no sign had been made by the King of acceding to the important demand that he should surrender himself to Her Majesty the Queen. The considerations which, with the lives of so many of his countrymen in Theodore's hands, had impelled Sir Robert Napier to impose this condition, had lost none of their force now. It was essential for the vindication of the national honour, which Theodore had so grossly insulted, that he should be removed for ever from his place. Moreover, the British army could not have reached Magdāla at that season unless it had been aided by the country. Kassai's supplies of flour had rendered it, for the time, independent of the failure of Zulla to furnish that commodity. The grain of Enderta and Agame had enabled its transport animals to live and advance; but this aid was given in the full belief that the British Commander would rid the people of Theodore, and had he failed in this, he might have had to fight his way out of the country. Theodore's failure to submit himself left no other course open than to proceed against him as an enemy. Reliable information reached Sir Robert Napier that the Abyssinian army was recovering from its defeat;* that many soldiers, who had been unable to return to Magdāla on the night of the 10th, had since rejoined their ranks, and that fresh defensive arrangements were being made. On Monday morning, accordingly, the British Commander prepared to attack the enemy's position.

The troops were accordingly paraded on the plain, at the foot of the mountain, ready to ascend. For the first time the force fell in in concentrated order. Hitherto the brigades had been separated, and so large a portion of men had been scattered along the line of baggage, that there had been no opportunity of seeing their real strength. The 33rd were now drawn up 750 strong; the 4th, 450; the 45th, 400. The whole of the Beloochees were present, as their left wing had arrived during the night, and the whole of the Punjabees; besides a detachment of the Royal Engineers, six companies of Sappers and Miners, and a detachment of the 10th Bombay Native Infantry. The cavalry was not present, as it had been sent to close the issues of Magdāla on all sides not held by the Gallas. There was a formidable force of artillery, however, with the troops, as Murray's Armstrong battery, two mountain batteries,

---

* Mr. Flad's statement.

the Naval Rocket Brigade, and two 8-inch mortars were available. The Armstrong guns and the two mortars, manned by a detachment of the 5th Battery of the 25th Brigade, were placed under the command of Lieutenant-Colonel Wallace, R.A., and took up a position, with Selassie in front and Fahla on the right, whence they could fire at long ranges, and aid the movements of the column, if the enemy should offer opposition to its advance up the hill to Islamgi; for Sir Robert Napier—who had first intended to assault Fahla from the side which fronted his camp, and was there screened from the fire of Selassie and Islamgi—under the altered condition of the enemy, when Theodore had, by death, wounds, or desertion, lost half of his army and his bravest chiefs, determined to attack Islamgi by the King's Road.

Before the troops were formed, intelligence was brought to Sir Robert Napier, that Theodore had left Magdála, which was confirmed by the appearance of several chiefs, with an offer to surrender into the hands of the British the two strong outposts of Fahla and Selassie, held by their people. He at once sent word to the Gallas, offering a reward of 50,000 dollars for Theodore's capture should he really have escaped. The scarcity of water had rendered it impossible to retain any considerable body of cavalry before Magdála. It was important, in case of an attempt by Theodore to fly from the fortress, that the western side should be immediately watched; and the personal escort of the Commander-in-Chief, with a few detached men of other corps, was sent, under command of Lieutenant Scott, A.D.C., to observe that quarter until the arrival of the main body of the cavalry (consisting of 3rd Dragoon Guards, Lieutenant-Colonel Tower; 3rd Bombay Cavalry, Captain Moore; 12th Bengal Cavalry, Major Gough), under Colonel Graves, who completed the investment to the Kaffir-bir Gate, which was watched by the Gallas. The Bashilo was held by the head-quarter detachment of the Sind Horse, under Major Briggs, and detachments of the 3rd Dragoon Guards, 3rd and 12th Cavalry, under Major Miller, to secure that point, and provide against the escape of the enemy by the Menchara ravine.

At seven o'clock a portion of the 3rd Bombay Cavalry and 12th Bengal Cavalry, mustering fifty sabres, under Lieutenant-Colonel Loch, were sent up to the Fahla saddle, and placed at the disposal of the Intelligence Department, to communicate with those of Theodore's troops which had surrendered.

Sir Robert Napier then ordered Sir Charles Staveley to advance on Islamgi, and occupy Fahla and Selassie, in the same order as had been designed for the assault, and without relaxing any of those precautions which had been considered necessary for the attack.

The three hills of Fahla, Selassie, and Magdála were each surrounded, at the top, by steep and precipitous scarps. Fahla and Magdála were joined to Selassie by saddles, and were nearly at right-angles to the central hill. A tolerably good, but in some places very steep, road led from the British camp up the north side of Fahla, over the saddle along the south of Selassie, and over the next saddle, Islamgi, into Magdála.* A pathway branched off this road at the Fahla saddle to the left, ran along the foot of the Selassie scarp for some distance, and then turned up a zigzag to the top, near the entrance to the fortress of Magdála. Another pathway led direct up to Selassie from the Fahla saddle. Neither of these paths were found practicable for mules, although they had been reported to be so. The summits of Fahla and Magdála were flat; that of Selassie sloped upwards from the scarp to the centre, and its summit commanded the two other mountains.

On the advance being ordered, at half-past 8 A.M., the Armstrong guns of Murray's Battery and the two 8-inch mortars were placed in their covering position; the mountain battery commanded by Lieutenant-Colonel Penn,† having ascended a short distance with the column, was placed in position on a spur on the left of the road, to cover the head of the ascent; whilst the mountain battery commanded by Captain Twiss,‡ followed in rear of the leading battalion of infantry.

---

* Report of Sir Charles Staveley.
† 'A' Battery 21st Brigade Royal Artillery.
‡ 'B' Battery 21st Brigade Royal Artillery.

Both mountain batteries were under the command of Colonel Milward. The division moved up the road with the 2nd Brigade, headed by a ladder-party of Sappers in front. The 2nd Brigade consisted of—

'B' Battery 21st Brigade Royal Artillery (Captain Twiss)	103 men.
'G' Battery 14th Brigade Royal Artillery (Capt. Murray)	94 ,,
Detachment of 5th Battery 25th Brigade Royal Artillery (Major Hills, V.C.)	27 ,,
33rd Regiment (Major Cooper)	694 ,,
Six companies 45th Regiment (Lieut.-Col. Parish)	325 ,,
Wing 10th Regiment Native Infantry (Colonel Field)	271 ,,

'It was a fine sight to see the long line of red, Royal Engineers (toiling under their scaling-ladders), Sappers, 33rd and 45th Regiments, the 4th King's Own in their grey kakee, the Beloochees in their dark green, the Royal Artillery in blue, and the mountain batteries on mules, winding up the steep and picturesque path that led to the Fahla saddle; while down the sides of the hill, by every sheep-track, streamed the soldiery of Theodore, who had surrendered to Captain Speedy, and laid down their arms. Old men and boys, mothers, and families with their household treasures, were seeking an asylum in the Arogi valley till the storm of war should be over above. Sword and helmet sparkled in the morning sun, the banners were unfurled, the breeze was just enough to display their gay colours and the proud names woven thereon, and all nature seemed to contribute to the splendour of the pageant.

'Inspirited as the soldiers were by the thought that

their toils were now almost over, and that success was about to crown their enterprise, their ardour was also strengthened by the uncertainty which surrounded everything up to the very last moment. For all anybody knew to the contrary, Theodore might have 10,000 armed men in battle-array on the top, or he might, as already reported, have died a suicide's death.'* For, as the column was ascending the mountain, contradictory statements were continually brought to Sir Robert Napier. Hardly had one messenger confirmed the report of his flight, than another would come with the information that he had returned to Magdāla, and was busily engaged in massacring the Abyssinian prisoners confined there, to be followed by a third, stating that he had committed suicide.

A company of the Belooch Battalion, under Lieutenant Beville, was sent up the first accessible spur on the right into Fahla, and was supported by two companies of the 10th Regiment of Native Infantry, which, under Colonel Field, climbed up the next spur.

About midday, the head of the column reached the Fahla saddle, when the advance-guard of two companies of the 33rd Regiment was pushed on to the summit of Selassie, supported by the remainder of the 2nd Brigade and Twiss's mountain battery; but the path was so bad that the mules could not accomplish it, and only three mountain-guns could be passed up, and those

* Shepherd's Campaign in Abyssinia.

by hand. When Selassie was crowned by the 2nd Brigade, the King's troops there were ordered to lay down their arms, and retire to the plain below. The first portion of this order was immediately obeyed: the people everywhere laid down their arms, and men women and children left the mountain as quickly as the narrow exit permitted. It was hardly possible to form a correct estimate of their numbers; they covered the whole face of the hill, and the paths leading from it were thronged for many hours during their migration. It was believed that the numbers could not have been less than from 25,000 to 30,000, of whom about a third were armed men.

The two hills of Fahla and Selassie formed a very strong position, and if they had been defended with ordinary determination, would have caused very serious loss of life in their capture. If only the women had kept behind the brows of the hills and rolled down stones, they might have destroyed many men before the summit could have been won. When they were secured, orders were sent for Lieutenant-Colonel Wallace to bring up Murray's Armstrong guns and the 8-inch mortars. This was accomplished by means of the elephants.

The state of matters in the actual stronghold of Magdála remained as much a problem as ever for the British Commander to solve. About noon, Theodore, with about a hundred picked followers, left the *amba* and went towards the market-place in Islamgi, where his guns were placed. These he intended to move into his citadel, and with them to defend it resolutely to the last.

At this time the detachment of Bombay Light Cavalry, under Colonel Loch, had emerged on the Islamgi saddle; and Sir Charles Staveley, seeing the advance of the Abyssinians from the fortress towards their guns, pushed down a company of the 33rd Regiment to the saddle, with orders to keep the guns under their fire. Theodore met these two detachments. He then called for his horse, and having mounted it, and ordered two of his guns to be dragged into Magdála, began careering about, boasting of his prowess, firing off his rifle as a challenge, and calling on a champion to come out and meet him. He did not, however, come sufficiently far to allow Colonel Loch to intercept his retreat to the fortress, and the latter had to rest content to prevent, by the fire of his infantry, the King or his followers making their escape by any path leading down from the Islamgi saddle. A desultory fire from small guns was meanwhile maintained from the defences of the fortress against the detachment, which was answered by turning some of Theodore's own guns against him, when he withdrew to where his people were engaged in dragging the guns towards the gate of the fortress. Several round-shot fell near him; still his men did not abandon the guns, until a rifle-bullet from the infantry killed one of them. All then retired into the *amba*, and the gate was closed.

A pause then ensued, when the few troops on the Islamgi saddle perceived a dreadful stench. The cause was now apparent. At the foot of the precipice, on their right, lay, in one putrefying mass, the Galla prisoners, whom Theodore had massacred on the 9th and thrown over the rock. They lay there, in an advanced state of corruption, old men, women, and children—some manacled, and a few chained together. This sight of wholesale slaughter caused a deep feeling of hatred to Theodore among the British soldiery.

The British Commander in the meantime reconnoitred Magdála, and prepared for the attack of the fortress. Beyond the saddle of Islamgi, the rock of Magdála rose in a steep scarp, three hundred feet in height. A double line of defence, in each of which was a narrow gate, crowned the scarp; to these a steep, narrow, and rugged path led up. Whatever number of defenders the fort contained was studiously concealed; it was plain, however, that the place was not abandoned, as the gates, which had at first been open, were closed, and figures of armed men could occasionally be seen in the *amba*, one of which was believed to be that of Theodore.

About 1 P.M. the Commander-in-Chief ordered a tolerably sharp cannonade to be directed on the gate.

No one of the assailant force could tell what was the amount of fire which the fortress then gave forth, as the noise was drowned by the British artillery, but had it not been for this cannonade few would have passed up the ascent and reached the gateway alive. Many armed men were lurking behind the defences, as the heaps of arms found when the place was taken proved. The three mountain-guns on Selassie fired a few rounds from that position, when it was found that the clearness of the atmosphere and the grand proportions of the mountains had led to the distances being underrated, and Colonel Milward was ordered to place the three other guns of Twiss's battery with Penn's battery in a better position at the foot of Selassie, and directly opposite the gate of Magdāla, from which they were 1,300 yards distant. The three guns were therefore moved down from Selassie, so that Lieutenant-Colonel Milward had a formidable battery of twelve guns, supported by four rocket-tubes, under his supervision. The cannonade did not elicit any demonstration from the fortress, and the Commander-in-Chief, in consideration of the women and children who were known to be in Magdāla, did not ever advance his artillery beyond this position, whence it could fire on the defences without doing serious damage within the interior of the *amba*.

By order of Sir Robert Napier, Sir Charles Staveley then made dispositions for the assault of the fortress by the 2nd Brigade, supported by the 1st, which had advanced along the lower road after Selassie had been occupied by the 2nd Brigade.

The 33rd Regiment, ten companies strong, were to advance across Islamgi, two companies being in skirmishing order, and two in support; the remaining six companies, under Major Cooper, headed by a detachment of the Royal Engineers, under Major Pritchard, and the 'K' Company of Madras Sappers and Miners, under Captain Elliot, with powder-bags, crowbars, and ladders, were to form the storming-party. Two companies of Bombay Sappers and Miners, under Captain Leslie and Lieutenant Leacock, were to follow in rear of the 33rd Regiment. On nearing the foot of the steep ascent up to the gate of the fortress, the skirmishers were to halt, and, reinforced by the supports, maintain a steady fire upon the gate and the defences during the ascent of the storming-party. The 45th Regiment, under Lieutenant-Colonel Parish, was to advance in line in rear of the 33rd Regiment, and the 1st Brigade—with the exception of the Punjab Pioneers, and two companies of the 10th Native Infantry, which had been left to guard the camp at Arogi, some distance in rear—was to move up in column as a reserve. Two companies of the 10th Native Infantry, under Colonel Field, were to remain on Selassie, to guard the arms surrendered by Theodore's troops, and clear the Abyssinians off the mountains. The Armstrong guns and 8-inch mortars, which had arrived on elephants from below, were to advance along the main road, south of Selassie, as far as practicable, and cover the advance of the infantry, while the two mountain and naval rocket batteries at the foot of Selassie were to keep up a fire upon the gate of the fortress.

About 3 P.M. the batteries opened fire, and the shells from the mountain-guns fell thick upon the gateway and the adjoining defences. The Armstrong guns and mortars did not reach so good a position as that of the mountain batteries, as it was impracticable, on account of the nature of the ground, to advance them farther than within 2,400 yards of the gate. Nevertheless, Captain Murray threw some shells with good effect; but Major Hills fired only a few rounds from his mortars, as he found that his position was not sufficiently far advanced to produce a great result. The fire of the artillery was concentrated against the gateway and the north end of the fort, which was crowded with the houses of the soldiers, avoiding as much as possible the higher parts of the interior, occupied by the Abyssinian prisoners and non-combatants. During the cannonade the enemy carefully concealed themselves from view, so that the place seemed almost deserted, although, when entered by the troops, it was found to be thronged with soldiers, who had thrown away their arms, released prisoners, and the numerous voluntary and involuntary followers of Theodore's fortunes.

About 4 P.M. the advance to storm was ordered. The mountain batteries as long as possible kept up a fire over the heads of the troops advancing to the assault. The 33rd Regiment, led by Major Cooper, and keeping up a continuous fire from its skirmishers, soon surmounted the steep precipitous cliff which lay between it and the outer gate, notwithstanding the fire of the garrison from behind its first defensive line, which consisted of a wall surrounded by strong and thick barricades of thorny stakes, with a narrow stone gateway. On arriving at the gateway, the progress of the assailants was arrested, for it was closed, and, for the moment, the engineers had not at hand the powder-bags with which to blow it in. The crowbars were, however, set to work, and the gate was broken down, when it was found that the path of the gateway, fifteen feet deep, was filled up with large stones to a height of twelve feet, which formed an almost insurmountable obstacle. While the Sappers were engaged upon the gate, the garrison maintained a constant fire upon them through their loopholes, and during that time nine officers and men received wounds or contusions. Meanwhile, some of the men of the 33rd, turning to the right, found a point where the wall and fence were sufficiently low to be surmounted by means of a scaling-ladder. Here they entered, and, taking the defendants of the gate in flank, drove them up a narrow path, which, twisting through rocks and soldiers' huts, led to another narrow gateway, some seventy yards higher up. Through this the leading men of the 33rd rushed, close behind the rearmost fugitives; and being followed by the whole regiment, the summit of the fortress was quickly occupied, the standard of England was planted upon the African rock which had so long been the prison-home of British envoys, and Magdāla was captured. The followers of Theodore immediately threw down their arms and prayed for quarter, which was of course granted, and no further loss of life occurred.

This fortress, which was comparatively easily carried, was one of the strongest, even when its own proper defences were reached, which could be found in the world. Its position with reference to its outworks, Fahla and Selassie, adds so much to its strength that it might be made quite impregnable. If Theodore had been properly supported by his soldiers, the British could not have escaped severe loss in its attack. As it was, however, his army had been so completely demoralised by the severity of the loss fortuitously inflicted on them two days before, that the troops remaining faithful to Theodore were few; and when they found that their unscientific defences gave them no opportunity to inflict loss on the assailants, without exposing themselves to the fatal effects of the rapid fire of the breechloaders, they abandoned the contest as soon as their first line of defence was carried by the stormers.

Among the dead at the outer gateway were found several of Theodore's devoted chiefs; among others Ras Engedda, who had endeavoured to persuade him to massacre his European prisoners. The body of Theodore was found some way up the path which led from the second gateway to the palace. It appeared that Theodore,* after re-entering Magdála when fired upon by Colonel Loch's detachment, had ordered the gateway to be filled up with stones, and had himself set the example in the work. When the British artillery opened, he and his followers remained under cover, and few of the three hundred well-armed men whom he had with him were injured, but Ras Engedda was killed by a shell just inside the gate. When Ras Engedda fell, Theodore himself hurried farther up the fortress, divested himself of the gold-brocaded mantle which he had worn early in the day, and which he seemed to think made him a mark for the aim of the guns, and gave it to a servant. As soon as the storming party carried the outer gate, he exclaimed to those near him, 'Flee! I release you from your allegiance. As for me, I shall never fall into the hands of an enemy.' Drawing his pistol, he put it into his mouth, fired, and fell dead. His immediate followers fled

* Statement of Theodore's servant.

across the *amba*, and went out of the Kaffir-bir Gate; but were confronted by the Gallas, who tauntingly invited them to approach. Debarred from escape, they crept into a cave; but hearing, in the evening, that the British did not kill their prisoners, they came in and surrendered themselves.

Immediately on entering the fortress the Commander-in-Chief made a rapid examination of the interior, and ordered a guard to be placed on the Kaffir-bir Gate, the approaches to which from the interior were choked with arms thrown aside apparently in hasty flight. As the owners could not have passed the Gallas, many must have returned to swell the crowd within the fortress.

Groups of huts thickly crowded together, and many of them occupied, gave room for dangers of a nocturnal conflagration, or acts of violence.

The only way of meeting this difficulty was to collect all the Abyssinians, except the Royal Household, in the open space in the centre of the fortress, where they could be cared for and protected; they quickly hutted themselves, and remained there until they could be sent away.

Early on the morning of the 13th, the main body of the cavalry, under Colonel Graves, moved from the Bashilo, and marching to the south side of Magdála, threw out picquets to watch all the avenues leading from the fortress between the British camp at Arogi and the Kaffir-bir Gate, which was watched by the Gallas. The regiments employed on this duty consisted of the head-quarters of the 3rd Dragoon Guards, under Lieutenant-Colonel Tower, the 3rd Bombay Cavalry, and 12th Bengal Cavalry; while, at the same time, the fords of the Bashilo were watched by picquets of the same regiments, placed under the charge of Major Miller, of the 3rd Dragoon Guards. The cavalry picquets were within reach of each other, and were kept in constant communication by means of frequent patrols, so that before the assault the fortress was closely invested, and Theodore was deprived of all hope of escape. The next day the cavalry returned to its former position on the Bashilo; it had not come in contact with the enemy, and suffered no casualties in men, but lost not a few horses from the cold to which it was subjected, and from the insufficiency of grain, under which it had long suffered during several forced marches.

The whole of Theodore's guns were captured at the same time as his fortress. They consisted of—

```
3 brass 56-pounders smooth-bore.
1   "   18      "           "
4   "    6      "           "      Turkish.
4   "    6      "           "
2   "    6      "           "      English (cast at Cossipore).
1   "    6      "           "      French.
5   "   24-pounder howitzers       Native and French.
3   "   12      "           "
1   "    3      "           "
4 iron   1      "           "
```

1 brass 20-inch   mortar
1   „   13 „   „
2   „   10 „   „
5   „   from 2¼ to 6-inch „

These guns, mortars, and howitzers were all found serviceable, and supplied with ammunition, except one 56-pounder, which had burst on the 10th. This ordnance was much superior, both in number of pieces and in calibre, to the artillery of the British; had it not been deserted by its gunners, it must have caused much loss to the assailants of Magdāla. Its existence proved the wisdom of the resolution of the British Commander to carry forward his Armstrong guns and mortars to the very entrance of Magdāla.

The British casualties at the storming of Magdāla were not very serious. Major Pritchard, R.E., received two wounds by splinters of stones; Corporal Hobson, a splintered wound of right leg; Sapper Denis, a slight splintered wound of forehead; Sergeant Jones and Private Lake, 33rd Regiment, were severely shot through the right leg; Privates Hayne, Daly, and Hickson, of the same regiment, received slight gunshot or spear wounds; one man of the Madras Sappers and one of the 3rd Light Cavalry also received severe gunshot wounds. Captain Elliot, of the Madras Sappers; Cornet Dalrymple, of the 19th Hussars, attached to the Madras Sappers; Sergeant Fielding, of the Madras Sappers; Sergeant Dean, R.E., and Lieutenant

Morgan, R.E., were also hurt near the gateway, but were not returned as wounded.*

The force that was engaged in the capture of Magdāla has been asserted by those ignorant of the exact circumstances to have been too large. Yet had Theodore held the summit of his mountain fastness and defended it properly with the weapons at his disposal, the force of the assailants would evidently have been rather inadequate for success; and had he sent a detachment to trouble the British communications with the Bashilo, his adversary would have been seriously inconvenienced. The Abyssinians were better armed than many of the adversaries who dispute with the British power in India. Double-barrelled percussion guns, which take life at the same distance as a musket, are weapons not

---

* Subjoined is a nominal roll of men wounded in the action at Arogi, which completes the list of wounded in the campaign:—

Captain Edward Roberts,	4th King's Own,	dangerously.
Sergeant M. Creedur	,,	,,
Private G. Kirby	,,	,,
,, G. Snifield	,,	slightly.
,, Deal Singh	23rd Punjabees	,,
Pioneer Basa Kall	,,	severely.
,, Kall Sing	,,	,,
,, Utter Sing	,,	dangerously.
,, Jewal Sing	,,	severely.
Bugler Kosal Sing	,,	,,
Private Jeeta Sing	,,	,,
,, Sunoop Sing	,,	slightly.
,, Goorun Sing	,,	,,
,, Heera Sing	,,	,,
,, Jewan Sing	,,	,,
,, Jawala Sing	,,	,,
Sapper C. H. Sumboo	,,	,,

to be despised. The force at the disposal of Sir Robert Napier was too small to allow him to attack at two points, nor could he have detached a column to threaten the farther side of the fortress without great risk.

Nor was a larger force available. The weakness of the posts along the line of communications is shown in the reports of the officers of the intelligence department, which demonstrate that the tension along that line was drawn to its utmost limit. At the time of the capture of Magdāla every station was beginning to be pressed. The robbers about Senafe from the Shoho country were becoming extremely daring. Several bodies of armed men hung upon the line between Senafe and Adigerat, and more than one convoy was molested. The detachment at Goona-goona had to turn out to repel an attack by an armed party; and the increase of such molestations obliged the Commander-in-Chief to order up a detachment of seamen to strengthen Senafe. At Adigerat the garrison was so much reduced that nothing but the two guns retained there maintained respect for it, and it was being mobbed when a detachment of the 25th Native Infantry opportunely arrived to reinforce it. Farther in advance, at Agula, the Mahommedan inhabitants were troublesome, and had the army been in trouble, the Gallas would have been called up to attack that post. Waldo Jasous was ever threatening the communications, at one time stopped the transport, and but for the force sent against him by Prince Kassai would probably have attacked the post at Atalo, or cut off that at Belago. The posts at Atalo, Makhan Ashangi, and Dildi had to turn out, and to fire upon the men of Waldo Jasous. The whole border population, whether Mahommedan or Christian, could not resist the sight and temptation of property.

It was a source of fear lest the small strength of the parties along the line of communications might tempt the people to attack them, and then, when blood was once well drawn, a feud would have ensued which would have led to a thorough interruption of the British convoys. The supplies obtained from the country were invariably in direct proportion with the strength of the troops; when these were weak they came in feebly. Those who were with the main body, where great strength was displayed, had no opportunity to estimate the hazards or dangers of the campaign.

The action of Arogi was anything but a skirmish against ill-disciplined or barbarous assailants. The ground was so covered with tangled brushwood and shrubs that the movements of regular armies were of little avail, and it was with difficulty that the British regiments escaped surprise in its broken and wooded configuration. The enemy sacrificed his great advantages when he descended to fight in the low ground instead of remaining on the hill, but even there he was repulsed not without skill and valour.

CHAPTER XIV.

DESTRUCTION OF THE FORTRESS.

AFTER the capture of Magdála, the command of the place was entrusted to Brigadier-General Wilby, who held it with the 33rd and a wing of the 45th Regiments. So thickly was the fortress inhabited, and so great was the crowd of people, that it was no easy matter to establish order. Guards were, however, placed at the gates, and at all points where protection was required.

The crown and royal seal of Theodore were taken possession of in the name of the Queen. A letter was addressed to his widow, in which Sir Robert Napier offered to accomplish her desires with regard to the disposal of the body. By her request, on the 14th, it was buried with all decency, but without military honours, in the Church of Magdála.

On the 15th the 4th (King's Own) Regiment relieved the 33rd in Magdála, and the 45th were removed to Islamgi, to reinforce the detachment of the 10th Native Infantry, engaged under Colonel Field in protecting the captured arms and ordnance. The inhabitants of Magdála were collected at Arogi, where great vigilance was necessary to protect them from the Gallas, who were lying in wait both day and night for opportunities of plundering or destroying them. Notwithstanding the friendly relations with the Queen of the Gallas, her people were so little under restraint that it was frequently necessary to fire upon them, to drive them off from molesting the water-parties and carrying away the mules. One party of them, in search of plunder, even dared to make their way into Magdāla, where they were captured by the guard of the 33rd Regiment.

Anxious as the British commander was to abstain from any further interference in Abyssinian affairs, after the object of the expedition had been attained, it was necessary, for the sake of the national credit, that due consideration should be shown for the large numbers whose interests and safety had centred in Theodore's existence, and who remained disarmed and unprotected, and exposed to merciless plunder and slaughter, at the hands of the wild tribes whom circumstances had for the moment converted into the allies of their conquerors. They included many women, and some had considerable property in goods and cattle. On the 15th and 16th they were told to move from Arogi, and go freely to their own districts, taking with them all that belonged to them. The defile from Arogi to the Bashilo was guarded for their protection by British infantry, and their march was escorted by patrols of cavalry as far as Bethor, where their safety from being plundered was assured. The disposal of the fortress of Magdála then demanded the attention of Sir Robert Napier. It is situated, geographically, within the territory of the Wallo Gallas, from whom it had been finally wrested by Theodore about ten years previously. In his hands it imposed an effectual check upon the encroachments of the Mahommedan Gallas in Christian Abyssinia. Sir Robert Napier desired, in the interests of Christianity, to place the stronghold in the possession of Wagshum Gobaze, the ruler and principal chief of the neighbouring portion of Abyssinia. A letter was accordingly sent to Gobaze, offering him the possession of the fortress; but, notwithstanding his repeated invitations to the British to come quickly to his aid, he had removed himself and his army to a distant quarter before the arrival of the English orce in front of Magdála. His lieutenant, Dejatch Mashesha, was however in the vicinity, and to him the place was offered for his master. Before his answer could be received several claimants applied for it. One of these was the Chief of Daont, and the two rival queens of the Gallas each solicited it for her own. Werkait first presented herself in the camp to press her claims, and was greatly affected in revisiting a locality which had been associated with so many misfortunes to her family and people. She said, 'We fought with Theodore as long as we could, and when his power was too strong for us to resist any longer, my son submitted to him on receiving a promise of good treatment, notwithstanding which he was inhumanly cut to pieces, and thrown over the precipice of Magdāla ; and now I have come to see the grave of my enemy Theodore, and the place where my son fell.' At this time the offer of the fortress had been made to Gobaze's lieutenant, and his answer had not been received. Magdāla was still in the possession of the British troops, and the scene of military operations, and the exodus of its former inhabitants was not completed; therefore it was not judged expedient that, at the moment, Werkait's desire to ascend the mountain should be indulged. Almost before her story was concluded intimation was received that her rival (Masteeat) was also in the neighbourhood, and on her way to offer her congratulations and submit her claim. Sir Robert Napier at first hoped to be able to make peace between these two rival queens; but when this was hinted at to Werkait, she said, 'When two persons are striving for a crown, how can peace be made between them? If Masteeat were to make peace with me to-day, before you, she would betray me to-morrow.' The news of Masteeat's approach caused great uneasiness among Werkait's escort and adherents; and after a second interview with the Commander-in-Chief, during which she exhibited symptoms of much distress, she took a hasty departure, apprehensive lest she should be intercepted by her more powerful and more fortunate rival —more fortunate because her son was alive, and the centre of the hopes of the large body of the people, while to Werkait there remained only the memory of her son, treacherously slain by Theodore.

Dejatch Mashesha arrived in camp, and in the name of Wagshum Gobaze declined to accept Magdála, alleging as his reason that it would require so large a garrison to hold it, that it would be a source of weakness rather than of strength. Masteeat shortly afterwards arrived with her son, Emam Ahmad, and expressed no small gratitude and rejoicing at Theodore's fall. She had responded very effectually to the request of Sir Robert Napier, to close all avenues by which Theodore could have escaped, and thus she came in the character of an established ally. To her request for the possession of Magdála, Sir Robert Napier was enabled to answer, that as Gobaze's lieutenant had declined to receive it, he would abandon the place after dismantling it, and burning all of it that could be so destroyed—as a mark of the anger of the British at the ill-treatment of their countrymen, as well as of their abhorrence of the cruelties which Theodore had committed there. To this the Queen replied that, indeed, nothing but fire could purify it. On being asked if she could make peace with Werkait, she answered that she would gladly do so, but that it was impossible, because if Werkait were to swear friendship on the Koran itself to-day, she would violate her oath to-morrow.

Advantage was taken of the friendly relations with Masteeat to obtain from her safe-conducts, and the promise of protection, for as many of the people of Magdála as had occasion to pass through Galla territory on their way home, as well as for the care of some of the Abyssinians who had been wounded in the action of Arogi.

The elephants and heavier ordnance having been sent in advance on the 15th, on the 17th orders were issued for everyone to be cleared out of Magdála by 4 P.M. At that hour working-parties commenced the demolition of the captured ordnance, and the destruction of the fortress. The former were burst into atoms. The defences and gates of the *amba* were mined and sprung, and fire was applied to the palace and other houses, which spread quickly from habitation to habitation; these, burning slowly in the strong flame, sent up a heavy cloud of dense smoke, which could be seen for many miles.

On the 18th the last of the British force crossed the Bashilo on its homeward route, and encamped that evening on the Dalanta plain, while Masteeat lost no time in establishing herself and her followers in the dismantled fortress of Magdála.

On the 19th preparations were made for the return of the whole force to Zulla, and precautions taken to ensure the safety of the baggage and convoys, from the numerous robbers and marauders who hung upon the flanks and rear of the army, attempting on every occasion to plunder, and had to be frequently fired upon by the rearguard to prevent molestation from them.

A pioneer force, under the command of Major Chamberlain—and composed of one troop of the 3rd Light Cavalry, the 3rd and 4th Companies of the Bombay Sappers and Miners, and the head-quarter wing of the 23rd Punjab Pioneers—was to leave the camp on Dalanta plain on April 21, and proceed in advance of the force by regular marches to Antalo, repairing the road where required, and making it practicable for elephants and mules. The released captives were escorted by this force. The headquarters of the 1st division, with the 2nd brigade—composed of the 3rd Regiment Sind Horse, the 12th Bengal Cavalry, the Armstrong Battery, Twiss's Mountain Battery, the 8-inch mortars, the 2nd Company Sappers and Miners, the 33rd Regiment, the 45th Regiment, and the 10th Native Infantry—were to leave Dalanta camp the day after the pioneer force, and proceed to Antalo by regular marches, halting for one day at the Takkazie, Dildi, Ashangi, and Antalo; while the headquarters of the 3rd Native Infantry were to march from Dildi to Antalo, three days before the pioneer force arrived at the former station. The headquarters of the army with the 1st brigade—composed of the headquarter wing 3rd Dragoon Guards,

DESTRUCTION OF THE FORTRESS.

the 3rd Light Cavalry, Penn's Mountain Battery, the Naval Brigade, the 4th (King's Own) Regiment, the 10th Company of Royal Engineers, the Madras Sappers, one wing of the 23rd Punjab Pioneers, and the Beloochees—were to leave Dalanta the day after the 2nd brigade, and follow it by regular marches to Antalo. All detachments of regiments at different stations were to join their regiments as they passed through. The 2nd field hospital, with the wounded, moved with the pioneer force, and the 1st field hospital with the 1st brigade.

On Dalanta plain the captives released from Theodore's power, who belonged to other nationalities than the British, were finally handed over to the foreign officers who had been permitted to accompany the headquarters of the army during the expedition. The plunder taken in Magdála was sold by auction, and the proceeds of the sale distributed among the troops as prize-money. The campaign was also declared to be over, in the following General Order which the Commander-in-Chief issued to the force :—

Adjutant-General's Office, Head-Quarters' Camp,
Dalanta Plain, 20th April, 1868.

Soldiers and Sailors of the Army of Abyssinia! The Queen and the people of England entrusted to you a very arduous and difficult expedition—to release our countrymen from a long and painful captivity, and to vindicate the honour of our country, which had been outraged by Theodore, King of Abyssinia.

I congratulate you, with all my heart, on the noble way in which you have fulfilled the commands of our Sovereign!

You have traversed, often under a tropical sun, or amidst storms of rain and sleet, four hundred miles of mountainous and rugged country.

You have crossed ranges of mountains (many steep and precipitous), more than ten thousand feet in altitude, where your supplies could not keep pace with you.

In four days you passed the formidable chasm of the Bashilo, and, when within reach of your enemy, though with scanty food, and some of you even for many hours without either food or water, you defeated the army of Theodore, which poured down upon you from its lofty fortress in full confidence of victory.

A host of many thousands have laid down their arms at your feet.

You have captured and destroyed upwards of thirty pieces of artillery, many of great weight and efficiency, with ample stores of ammunition.

You have stormed the almost inaccessible fortress of Magdala, defended by Theodore and a desperate remnant of his chiefs and followers.

After you forced the entrance to his fortress, Theodore, who himself never showed mercy, distrusted the offer of it held out to him by me, and died by his own hand.

You have released not only the British captives, but those of other friendly nations.

You have unloosed the chains of more than ninety of the principal chiefs of Abyssinia.

Magdala, on which so many victims have been slaughtered, has been committed to the flames, and now remains only a scorched rock.

Our complete and rapid success is due—firstly, to the mercy of God, whose Hand, I feel assured, has been over us

DESTRUCTION OF THE FORTRESS.

in a just cause; secondly, to the high spirit with which you have been inspired!

Indian soldiers have forgotten the prejudices of race and creed to keep pace with their European comrades.

Never did an army enter on a war with more honourable feelings than yours. This it is that has carried you through so many fatigues and difficulties; your sole anxiety has been for the moment to arrive when you could close with your enemy.

The remembrance of your privations will pass away quickly; your gallant exploit will live in history.

The Queen and the people of England will appreciate and acknowledge your services; on my part, as your Commander, I thank you for your devotion to your duty, and the good discipline you have maintained throughout.

Not a single complaint has been made against a soldier, of fields injured, or villagers wilfully molested, either in person or property.

We must not, however, forget what we owe to our comrades who have been labouring for us in the sultry climate of Zoulla, the Pass of Koomaylee, or in the monotony of the posts which maintained our communications. One and all would have given everything they possessed to be with us; they deserve our gratitude.

I shall watch over your safety to the moment of your re-embarkation, and shall, to the end of my life, remember with pride that I have commanded you.

CHAPTER XV.

THE RETURN MARCH.

THE troops moved off as ordered, and on April 22, the Commander-in-Chief, with the last of the force, marched to the edge of the Jidda ravine, and on the 23rd reached Bethor. On the 24th he moved again to Abdakom, where he received in audience a large party of Abyssinians of note, who had been liberated from Theodore's prison-house on the fall of Magdála. The first was Birroo Gashoo, the Chief of Godjam, who bore on his enfeebled frame the marks of fourteen years of confinement in chains. The second was Dejatch Aria, Prince of Enderta, who is the maternal uncle of Kassai, Prince of Tigre. For many years before his imprisonment, he had waged war with Oobye for the supremacy in Tigre. Oobye defeated him, and, in 1855, Theodore defeated and dispossessed Oobye, and made Aria viceroy of Tigre. After some time, distrusting him, Theodore summoned him to Magdála, and made him a prisoner. The third was Wagshum Tiferri, who was said to be the hereditary Prince of Wag, and to have been the means of letting Gobaze escape from falling into the hands of Theodore, for which he was imprisoned by the king.

The whole of those who were liberated is shown in the subjoined list,* but these were the men of the most note present at Abdakom. To all the British commander spoke, urging upon them the necessity of peace in the present state of Abyssinia. These chiefs were dismissed, but the widowed queen of Theodore, with her son and two brothers, still remained as guests in the British camp. On the 26th the bottom of the Takkazie valley was reached, on May 3 Lat, on the 9th Antalo, and on the 10th Meshik. Here the Queen, who had been ever treated with universal courtesy, and who had been attended by Dr. Lumsdaine, the medical officer attached to the personal staff of the Commander-in-Chief, was reported to be seriously unwell. She was a daughter of Oobye, the former King of Tigre, who had been taken prisoner, with his whole family, by Theodore, about thirteen years previously. Oobye remained a captive until his death. He had been originally the hereditary ruler of the province of Semien, a mountainous district south of Tigre. His empire over the latter province had been acquired by conquest. Theodore took his daughter from prison, and married her while still a child; but her elevation by no means bettered the condition of her two brothers who had been her fellow-captives, who had never so much as seen their sister after her marriage till released from prison by the British.

* See page 271.

The two brothers of the widowed Queen now wished to return to their native province of Semien, but acknowledged that they could not there protect their sister, as they had neither arms nor money; and feared to take with them her child, Alamayou, in case that his life might be taken by any aspirant for the empire of Abyssinia. They were accordingly allowed to depart, while the Queen and her son still remained as guests in the camp.

The march from Dalanta to Antalo was trying, from the frequent severe storms of rain which appeared to accompany the columns, and from which the troops in some degree, and more especially the followers and transport animals, could not fail to suffer. The wild border-tribes of Abyssinians and Gallas, through whom the route lay from the Takkazie to Antalo, being very little under the control of their distant and almost nominal rulers, were perfectly well behaved in the advance, but finding by degrees the vulnerable points of the army, had been for some time making attacks upon the muleteers and camp-followers when they ventured far from their escorts, and on some occasions even on the armed soldiers. In the first instances some camp-followers were killed, and in the latter, the soldiers being driven to use their weapons, several Abyssinians and Gallas were killed and wounded. Considerable numbers of armed men, principally Gallas, watched the march from the hills, and, although restrained by the presence of the columns, made attempts on the line of baggage, but met with little success. Soldiers were freely interspersed along the line, and the rearguard from Marawa to Antalo was continuously under the command of an experienced officer, Lieutenant-Colonel Bray, of the 4th (King's Own) Regiment. This was a clear indication of what a force returning in difficulties would have experienced. In the friendly territory of Prince Kassai, the troops returned to marches made easy by the improved roads, and the increased supplies of articles of food, turned into great luxuries by a period of privations, which were stored in the fortified posts of Antalo and Adigerat.

At Antalo, arrangements were made for the return of the force to Senafe. As soon as the pioneer force, under Major Chamberlain, reached Antalo, the garrison of Antalo moved to Zulla. The portion of the force in rear of the pioneer force was divided into five columns and moved on Adigerat and Senafe. The 1st column left Antalo on May 11; it consisted of the 3rd Regiment of Sind Horse, the 10th Bengal Cavalry, Twiss's Mountain Battery, the 3rd and 4th Companies of Bombay Sappers and Miners, and the headquarter wing of the 23rd Punjab Pioneers. The 2nd column left Antalo on May 12; it consisted of the 12th Bengal Cavalry, one wing of the 33rd Regiment, and one wing of the 23rd Punjab Pioneers. The 3rd column marched from Antalo on May 13; it consisted of Murray's

Armstrong Battery, Hill's mortars, the headquarters of the 33rd Regiment, and the 'R' Company of the Madras Sappers. The 4th column marched on the 14th; it consisted of the 3rd Bombay Light Cavalry, Penn's Mountain Battery, the 2nd Company of Bombay Sappers and Miners, the headquarter wing of the 45th Regiment, and the headquarter wing of the 10th Native Infantry. The 5th column marched on the 15th; it consisted of the 3rd Dragoon Guards, the Naval Brigade, the 10th Company Royal Engineers, the 4th (King's Own) Regiment, and the Beloochees. The headquarters of the 1st division marched with the 4th column, while the Commander-in-Chief and headquarters' staff accompanied the 5th column. Each column took ten days' rations with it from Antalo, and five from Adigerat. The infantry carried their greatcoats and mess-tins. Accordingly, on the 15th, the rear of the force evacuated Antalo, and marched to Haik-Hellat, where a letter was received from Ras Guksa, the elder brother of Kassai, Prince of Tigre, requesting permission to visit the Commander-in-Chief. Being duly invited, he arrived, and was told that some munitions of war would be presented to Pince Kassai at Senafe. At Haik-Hellat the widow of King Theodore died in the British camp, from disease of the lungs. She had received every comfort that it was possible to afford her. Her body was attended out of camp by a guard of honour, and was buried by the priests of the Abyssinian creed in the church of Chelikut. Her son still remained with the Commander-in-Chief, and subsequently accompanied Sir Robert Napier to England.

On May 24, the Commander-in-Chief reached Senafe, where, on the 25th, a review of the troops was held in honour of Her Majesty's birthday. Prince Kassai was present, and in the afternoon paid the Commander-in-Chief a private visit. The following day a durbar was held, at which Kassai was received with a salute, and at which he was informed that six mortars and six howitzers, with 400 rounds of ammunition, had been sent for to Bombay, which would be handed over to messengers whom he might send to Zulla for them: he was also presented with 850 muskets and bayonets, 40,000 rounds of small-arm ammunition, and 28 barrels of gunpowder. Sir Robert Napier impressed upon him that these weapons were designed solely to aid him in the defence of his own country, and not in the invasion of that of his neighbours. On May 28, Kassai reviewed his troops, and, leading his horsemen himself, made them, to the number of two thousand, perform various movements, consisting chiefly of furious charges and personal tilts. The British army had released four chiefs of Tigre from Magdála, and brought them with it to Senafe. These were introduced to Kassai, and took an oath of allegiance to him on the Gospels—Kassai, in his turn, swearing that he would accord them his protection. He requested afterwards, in a private audience, that two or three Europeans might be left behind for three months, to teach his soldiery the use of their new weapons; but to this Sir Robert Napier replied, that the soldiers belonged to the Queen of England, and could not be left behind without her special orders, but that any of the men of Tigre whom Kassai would send to Aden, could there be taught how to use their guns.

The presents bestowed upon Prince Kassai were but a recognition of his friendly services towards the expedition. Through the failure of the Land Transport Corps, Sir Robert Napier found himself, on reaching Zulla, at the outset of the campaign, compelled to look to local resources for the supply of transport and commissariat requirements, to an extent which he had not intended, and which these resources proved very inadequate to meet. All that could then be done was to try to develope to the utmost such sources of supply as were within reach. It must be remembered how important time was, and that the delay of a fortnight, or even less, might have made the difference between the campaign being terminated before the rains or not. Owing in part to the ravages of locusts, the resources of Abyssinia had fallen so low, that special efforts were necessary before it was possible to purchase even the little food that it contained. This was one of other strong reasons which made it so desirable to establish friendly relations with Prince Kassai. Such relations were established at his first meeting with Sir Robert Napier, near Adabagi; during the second interview, at the same place, the Commander-in-Chief saw that the grain, which the Prince had on the previous day promised to collect, would be furnished with all the more certainty if he had cause to expect some tangible acknowledgment of his services. Sir Robert Napier, therefore, informed him that if he proved himself a true friend of Her Majesty, he would be rewarded in a way that would be useful in defending himself against his enemies, and that, although no promise could be made, it was hoped that guns suitable for mountain warfare might be given him by the Queen of England. Large quantities of grain and wheat and barley, to the value of about 10,000 dollars, were soon afterwards sent as a gift to Sir Robert Napier by the Prince himself, at a time when every load of flour was of great value; and the far more important supplies which, with his help, the Commissariat was able to purchase in the province of Enderta, during the halt at Antalo, enabled the advance beyond that position to be begun on the day it was. The assurance, therefore, which Sir Robert Napier conveyed to Kassai, near Adabagi, was as fully justified by the result as it appeared to him expedient at the time it was given. The cordiality and completeness, moreover, with which Prince Kassai, although pressed by Turkish intriguers to oppose the British advance, entered into the views of the British commander, by appointing some of his confidential chiefs as commissioners with the commanders of the troops in Tigre, tended greatly to secure peaceful intercourse with the people.

There is, however, another view of the subject which must be mentioned. The best hope of Abyssinia enjoying peace lay in its provinces becoming partitioned between at least two distinct rulers. Many circumstances, independently of the great size of the country itself, and the geographical barriers which subdivide it, support this view. Any attempt on the part of one chief to take possession of all Abyssinia, would not only lead to a long civil war, but would still leave room for a state of anarchy and disorder, if its object were attained. When the positions of the two men who govern Tigre and Lasta are considered, it does not appear likely that Kassai will ever attack Gobaze, unless carried away by too powerful chiefs, while it is only too probable that the ambition of Gobaze will extend itself to Tigre. Indeed, one of the motives of the latter in not coming to meet the British General, appeared to be that the latter might require from him a promise that he would not invade Tigre, which promise he was not prepared to make, or at all events to keep, and he feared that he might afterwards incur the resentment of England by breaking such a stipulation.

The four Tigrean chiefs who had been released from

Magdāla, had enjoyed influence in their own province under a former dynasty. Had they not been restored to their homes, they would have been exposed to danger of destruction by the Gallas, or have been driven to seek a refuge with Gobaze, who would have found them useful agents in any designs against Kassai. They were accordingly taken back to Tigre, but it was apparent that, though this course involved the lesser of two dangers, it might in the end prove a source of trouble to Prince Kassai. All that could be done towards securing their allegiance was done. At Senafe they solemnly took oath, before the Prince, that they would be faithful to him, and Kassai as solemnly promised, in return, to afford them his protection. But this ceremony might or might not have the effect of restraining them from intrigues against him. Therefore, as the British restored them to a place in his dominions, they were bound to strengthen him against insurrection on their part. Had the British left a ruler whom they had found just struggling into power, and whose first use of that power had been for their assistance, exposed to pressing dangers when they could materially add to his means of self-defence by a gift, which was as nothing compared to their own resources, they would have adopted a course foreign to the characteristic policy of their country towards weaker States, even if hopes of the acknowledgment of his services had not been held out to him.

On May 29, the last of the British troops evacuated Senafe. The Commander-in-Chief was accompanied by Prince Kassai to the head of the pass, where the troops composing the rearguard were formed up, while a salute was fired in honour of the Prince, who shortly afterwards took leave of Sir Robert Napier, and returned towards Senafe. All local information had led to the belief that there would be no danger of floods in the Sooro Pass before the middle of June; but, owing to the extraordinary severity of the spring-rains, a succession of floods, during the early part of May, did much damage to the road through the defile. On May 19, with hardly any warning, a heavy flood, coming from a lateral tributary which enters the pass above Sooro, filled the channel of the Sooro defile so suddenly, that seven camp-followers and some cattle, not being instantly removed from the waterway, were swept away and perished. These losses were, however, due to a neglect of the precautionary instructions, which Sir Robert Napier had issued so early as the end of January, to secure the safety of the troops in the pass. By the exertions of the garrison of Sooro, the damage to the road in the pass was rapidly repaired after each flood.

On May 28, Mr. Dufton, who had been attached to the Intelligence Department, was attacked by a party of Shohos in the Koomayli Pass, and wounded so severely that death resulted. It is much to be regretted that he disregarded the stringent orders in force against anyone marching without an escort. Possibly he thought his position allowed him a certain degree of latitude in arranging his own movements. No doubt, also, his having travelled a good deal in Abyssinia, and his being so well known as he was amongst the Shohos, had made him less careful of his safety than he otherwise would have been. He had been able to render, in a quiet unobtrusive way, no inconsiderable service to the expedition, chiefly in the important work of assisting the Commissariat to purchase supplies from the people. His character had gained him the respect of everyone with whom he was associated, and when his remains were interred, in a suitable spot at Maiyen Wells, it was felt by all that the force had lost an useful and deserving officer.

On June 1 the Commander-in-Chief, with the last column of the Abyssinian Expeditionary Force, passed through the Sooro defile and reached Koomayli. On the following day he arrived at Zulla, where the embarkation of troops, stores, and animals had been busily progressing. The troops destined for England were despatched to Suez, thence by rail to Alexandria, and by troop transports home. The native regiments, and those Europeans who had not completed their period of service, returned to India. On June 10, Sir Robert Napier, after handing over to the Egyptian Governor, Abdul Kadir Pacha (who offered to take charge of them), the care of some railway plant and buildings which could not conveniently be removed till after the monsoon, and the custody of the British cemetery at Zulla, embarked in the 'Feroze,' and sailed for Suez, whence he was conveyed to England, having accomplished the objects of the expedition to the glory and honour of England, to the admiration and envy of Europe, without interference with the rights of any of the princes or chiefs of Abyssinia except Theodore, and having left Abyssinia with a fairer prospect of enjoying tranquillity than the country possessed when the British army first disembarked on the coast of the Red Sea.

The Abyssinian Expedition, and the relief of the captives held by Theodore, was not achieved without cost of money.

For this England should however have been prepared, as Sir Robert Napier perceived that the expense must be considerable, and when first consulted, having no expectation of commanding the expedition, for which he had recommended another officer, emphatically warned the Government on July 33, in these words :—

'It is hardly necessary to observe that no such expedition could be carried out without very great expenditure, and that the very best arrangements may be crippled by some misplaced economy.'

Again, on August 31, a minute written in reply to one from the Governor of Bombay :—

'One great and indispensable want is land transport, which can only be delivered at the point of action at a very vast expenditure.'

Under other circumstances the expenditure might be in the transport of great masses of artillery and gigantic siege trains.

The cost of the highly perfected ammunition of the present day expended in the course of a month's siege would be enormous; here our expense must be in the transport and maintenance of beasts of burthen, and if the British Government consider it necessary to prosecute the expedition, I conclude that the expenditure must be incurred, even if it be necessary to transport a considerable part of our baggage cattle from India.

The expense was however greater than the Commander-in-Chief anticipated, because the Government of Bombay, whether in the belief that Theodore would surrender his prisoners on the first threat of an invasion, or that they would be wrested from his grasp by the successes of rebels over him, or from some other cause, did not at the first take sufficiently energetic and vigorous measures.

The failure in the early part of the expedition proved the justice of the Commander-in-Chief's views, but materially increased the cost of the expenditure.

The transport corps improved greatly in the course of a few months, but the loss of time was irreparable.

The Punjab divisions, formed of men who were already disciplined and organised during their long march to the coast, were far more satisfactory, and were at once brought to the front.

Other causes led to the increase of expenditure.

Whether the Bombay Government were credulous of the assertions of those who believed that Theodore would be terrified by the presence of even a single British soldier at Massowah, or whether supplies were not procurable at such short notice, they did not arrive sufficiently early.

There was undue economy in taking up vessels, so that captains of ships which could at first have been easily available, left the port with other freight, and vessels were not forthcoming when subsequently required.

The supplies were not despatched to the force as quickly as they should have been. While four thousand transport animals were uselessly nourished at Bombay, the army which required them, and eagerly entreated their advent, was obliged to purchase animals in Abyssinia and Berbera.

The railway gear was old, of inferior material, and could not be laid rapidly for want of a sufficient number of experienced plate-layers.

The want of a proper department to superintend the

embarkation of stores at Bombay caused considerable expense of time and money.

The warm clothing sent from England was left in the commissariat stores at Bombay, instead of being sent to Zulla; this was pointed out to the Government, and a steamer was detained to take it on, but it was not sent in her, and substitutes had to be purchased from the stores of the men-of-war and transports.

The early recommendations of Sir Robert Napier for lighterage and cranes were not early attended to, and at first three cotton-boats were all that were sent to Annesley Bay with which to accomplish the landing of the material and supplies of an army; while an officer of the Marine Department, who, in his anxiety for the result, purchased six barges, was ordered to be held personally responsible for their cost, as at first one alone was sanctioned.

These circumstances, whether due to the idea that Theodore would readily surrender his captives, or to a well intentioned, but mistaken idea of economy, led to an unwillingness to submit promptly and energetically to a primary expense, and entailed in the end increased expenditure, losses, and delay, which no subsequent energy or exertion could remedy.

Much expense would have been saved if the Government of India had been content to furnish regiments in relief of the Bombay corps required for the campaign, instead of pressing to send them to the theatre of operations and incurring the excessive cost of transports from Calcutta. While, however, there may have been some lapses of foresight in India, in England the Commander-in-Chief was implicitly trusted. Of this trust he proved himself worthy, and the result justified the confidence reposed in him.

THE RETURN MARCH.

Roll of the Principal Chiefs liberated from Magdāla, showing the Length of their Imprisonment, and where they went to after Release.*

No.	NAMES	LENGTH OF IMPRISONMENT	POSITION AND COUNTRY	WHERE GONE TO
		Years		
1	Faris Alee	11	Chief of Edjoo	Rebelled temporarily, but probably submitted to Gobaze
2	Wagshum Tiferri	4	Chief of Wag, cousin of Wagshum Gobaze	Went to Gobaze to submit
3	Dejaz Sahelo	5	Chief of Haramat	Joined Kassai, and submitted to him at Senafe
4	Ajaj Negussy	5	Chief of Haramat, son of Sahelo	Remained at Haramat
5	Balgeda Muro	5	Chief of Tera	Remained at Dongolo
6	Shum Agame Aragavi	7	Chief of Agame	⎧ Joined Kassai of Tigre,
7	Lij Sahaja	5	Chief of Id	⎨ and submitted to
				⎩ him
8	Shum Salova Ezekias	5	Chief of Salowa	Went to Samnil
9	Dejaj Iman	15	Brother of Ras Ali	Left Magdāla, without paying his respects
10	Burroo Gosh, and two brothers	15	Chiefs of Godjam	Joined Gobaze, and submitted to him
11	Cassa, son of Dobey	14	Chief of Semien	⎫ Brothers of the Empress; went to Semien
12	Gwangul, son of Id	14	Chief of Id	⎭
13	Hugla Dereso	3	Chief of Selemh	Left Argee sick; destination unknown
14	Goshu Wondia	4	Chief of Belessa	Went to his country
15	Ras Walda Mariam	1	Chief of Begemder	Ditto
16	Ras Gebrie	1	Chief of Id	Ditto
17	Ras Waheda Tadla	1	Ditto	Ditto
18	Betwaded Tadla, and two brothers	1	Ditto	Ditto
19	Engeda	Unknown	Chief of Dembea	Ditto
20	Maureme	2	Chief of Shoa	Went to his country under safe-conduct of Masteeat, Queen of the Gallas
21	Ubié	2	Ditto	Ditto
22	Aregi, son of Sewale Sellassie	2	Ditto	Ditto
23	Ajah Wondie	1	Chief of Begemder	Went to his country
24	Ajaj Geret	3	Ditto	Ditto
25	Ajaj Gebra Selassie	1	Dttto	Ditto
26	Belala Gobazye	1	Ditto	Ditto
27	Sergie Deresso	1	Ditto	Ditto
28	Lej Meshasho	Unknown	Ditto	Ditto
29	Wossen Illma	1	Chief of Kwara	Ditto
30	Wossen Dareya	1	Chief of Id	Ditto
31	Pasha Hayle	10	Chief of Meja	Unknown
32	Talef Engeda	1	Chief of Tigre	Joined Kassai of Tigre, and submitted to him
33	Ras Lebie	3	Chief of Maga	Went to Shoa
34	Balgida Area	13	Chief of Enderta	Joined Kassai of Tigre, and submitted to him

* There were several others of Shoa and Waag, whose names are unknown, and of minor importance.

www.ingramcontent.com/pod-product-compliance
Lightning Source LLC
Chambersburg PA
CBHW020833160426
43192CB00007B/627